Regenerating Local Churches

Revd Maggie Durran, after several years as a vicar on the Old Kent Road in Walworth, south London, began to exercise her gifts and ministry in working with churches all over London on their buildings. For the past five years, as part-time historic churches project officer for the Diocese of London and as a freelance development and fundraising consultant she has worked with churches with building problems of many kinds. The result is a keen perspective on the challenges of church buildings and a wide experience of good management practice and the problem-solving solutions adopted in a variety of churches.

A regular columnist in the *Church Times*, Maggie Durran also leads seminars and workshops on various aspects of practical church management.

Regenerating Local Churches

Mission-based strategies for transformation and growth

Maggie Durran

CANTERBURY
PRESS
Norwich

First published in 2006 by the Canterbury Press Norwich
(a publishing imprint of Hymns Ancient & Modern Limited,
a registered charity)
9–17 St Alban's Place, London N1 0NX

www.scm-canterburypress.co.uk

British Library Cataloguing in Publication data

A catalogue record for this book is available
from the British Library

ISBN 1-85311-695-5/
978-1-85311-695-7

Typeset by Regent Typesetting, London
Printed and bound in Great Britain by
William Clowes Ltd, Beccles, Suffolk

Contents

Contents

Contents

Major presentation to all stakeholders
Review revenue projections with church council
Set up a management or steering committee for the
ongoing project

How to Use this Book

Setting out a process for a major programme such as regenerating a church identifies the basic steps through which churches will need to go whether the change they make is large or small. This book, through Chapters 6 to 9, is set out as a Development Cycle broken into many smaller steps. For convenience the descriptions cover the most complex plans; but even small projects in small churches will benefit from the systematic approach that asks all the basic preparatory questions before designing or building a project. The first Cycle of Development indicates a number of steps in exploring possibilities; the second Cycle outlines designing and planning – not just for architectural feasibility but for financial and staffing provision; the third Cycle covers the steps involved in activating the plan.

Many of the steps included in this systematic process are essential to every project though they may at times have been approached intuitively. For example, the discipline of completing the Option Appraisal will broaden the understanding of everyone connected with the project, reducing the possibility of the project appearing to be the 'baby' of one person or a small group.

The book suggests creating a team of people to steer the church through the regeneration stages. The church that does not have people available for a team may find it advisable to recruit non-churchgoers to some roles, or to recognize that with fewer people available and therefore less skills and time it may be better to keep to a relatively simple project.

Try first taking a look at all the sections and get a feel for their scope, then make a more considered study noting how each might or might not apply to your church. Once a team of people is established the process should be owned by all members, and each may wish to make their own notes from the book so that the process is understood by everyone.

The outline of the process you will follow includes the following stages:

- Assess the need for change
- Present the case for change (an excellent discipline, even if everyone in the church agrees change is necessary, in preparing for communication with people outside the church)
- Create a Team

- **Cycle One: Explore the possibilities**

  - Gather information
  - Consult people inside and outside the church
  - Review what's been gathered
  - Present to the Church Council

- **Cycle Two: Design and Plan**

  - Gather information, review what's been learned and create a strategy
  - Consult within and outside the church to consolidate partnerships
  - Update and consolidate information into a business plan
  - Present to the Church Council

- **Cycle Three: Activate the Plan**

Part 1

Introduction

1

Introduction

Worship

Worship is about God and giving God what is due to God, and is embodied in the encounter with God in worship services and the Eucharist. Mission is about getting new people to come to church and engage with God. Evangelism is about building up the body of Christ, quality as well as quantity; making mature Christians out of newcomers is not always a 'conversion' message, it involves encouraging and developing greater commitment to discipleship and ministry. Ministry is service to others, and is primarily about working for and with people in the neighbourhood or parish. Welcoming the stranger means working with and for those with whom the church has no connection or loyalty, although you and they live in the same neighbourhood. Many are local residents, some are homeless, some refugees, and more and more are believers in other faiths and ways to God.

Worship should enable a very wide variety of people to encounter God, not just 'people like us'. So the way that worship is planned and enacted should not only be suited to the preferences of the present congregation but open to the possibility of spiritual engagement with those who live, work or visit in the area. There are city churches with lunchtime weekday services, churches with Saturday evening services and a host of other variations. Some are traditional in style with organ and classical music, others use contemporary music with a band or keyboard. Mission will encourage us to expand to become inclusive.

Styles of worship

Many churches have developed skills in engaging with a variety of people at the same time, and with a varied programme: children, youth, adults, and older people. Is the shrinking church delivering something local people don't want, and can it deliver something they do want? If people don't already attend church they may well not know what would attract them, and clearly what the church is doing now is not drawing them in, so it may be time to try new ways of worship, or special events and new ways of communicating about church and God. In my experience many people under the age of 30 have never been inside a church let alone to a worship service, and encouraging them to come in and find a place requires a significant programme of enculturation. And the steps on the way have to avoid discouraging them; we should see that we open up possibilities in worship for them, and not just require them to conform. One church asked me about noisy children in the crêche area: how they could get them to play quietly while the service continues. Encouragement to listen for God and join in the service, using the play area only for difficult moments, is a positive way forward. It will require communication and an invitation, possibly at the beginning of the service, so newcomers, adults and children, join in the service and use the crêche as an occasional quiet area when a child is fractious.

Re-engagement with local people around the occasional offices can create bridges into the neighbourhood. New services for special occasions make another opportunity for people to engage with the spiritual and find their way to encounter God; an example is the Taizé-style service that has so much appeal for young people.

Serving local people

Many churches adapt their buildings to create space for much-needed activity with local people, such as providing a community hall or welfare projects that meet the needs of local people.

Turning the tide

But where the church is on a downward spiral, continuing to do what it already does is not an answer, as with the best will it has got itself onto the present slippery slope that way; only change offers the possibility of reversing the slide. What has usually happened is a drift away from effectiveness, and as culture around the church has changed, the church has worked harder at staying the same – perhaps a bit of a security blanket! Eventually there is very little synchronicity between the focus of the church and the culture, concerns and lifestyles of local people. There has to be new engagement and change to bring life.

Dislocation such as urban redevelopment of estates may have caused a cataclysmic break in patterns of local life that previously had the church engaged at its heart. For these churches it a question of finding a new purpose that is appropriate to the new context.

> One church in east London, a beautiful Grade I listed church, was surrounded and hidden by medium-rise blocks of flats, and the church entrance road became the entry to car-parking areas and bin bays. Not surprisingly the building, once the pride and joy of its members and local residents, lost all its local support as people were rehoused further away, and for new residents the church is virtually invisible and appears abandoned. New initiatives are being sought to find a new community that will use and treasure the church.

> Another London church, Grade I listed, lost its local streets in low-rise development that became the borough's sink estate – a place to house difficult families and individuals. The remaining small and loyal congregation was further split over controversy on the ordination of women and was further decimated. Today a struggling group tries to work with the new vicar to turn it around and make it thrive again. Change is essential, re-engagement with the neighbourhood is the route that is being taken.

Regeneration

Church regeneration brings together all our resources, all our history, our relationship with God, our paths to the sacred, our relationships with neighbours and strangers, and in the melting-pot we seek to develop something vital and encouraging for the ongoing church and for the many unchurched people among whom we live. A colleague of mine wrote in his church newsletter recently, as the church embarked on its own programme of re-engagement, 'While we are repairing and preserving our heritage, we are doing it as part of our responsibility for bringing the good news of God's love to our generation, and leave it in good order for the future generations.'[1]

---

[1] Venerable Bill Jacob, Archdeacon of Charing Cross and Rector of St Giles-in-the-Fields.

2

Challenging Churches

Targeting churches that need extra support is a challenge facing almost every diocese and denomination. My experience is most extensively in Anglican churches but other denominations face similar issues. If we can identify the churches that need extra support or more support in establishing a strategy for becoming active in mission and ministry, and thereby sustainable, we are talking far more than just survival. We could emphasize mission alone and encompass new developments in both evangelism and social engagement with the neighbourhood and still not be financially sustainable; but if we keep these issues together – mission, ministry and money – we can manage our developments to effectively achieve all our targets.

It is very difficult to actually determine that a church is failing, as normally we find that even in struggling churches there are people for whom it is the centre of their lives where a lifetime of faithful Christianity has been lived out, and to declare their church a failure is a nonsense. If the church is closed, few make a satisfactory transition to another church, that is unless the transition is well prepared and well executed.

Organizations, and charities, are increasingly familiar with this process, do sink to rather murky lows in their normal life cycle and many do re-emerge from the doldrums with new energy and renewed vision. So will most of our churches. But in renewing growth and development, we can simultaneously deal with the financial burden that almost all churches have experienced in the past two or three decades.

First, we must recognize those churches that are sliding

downwards, and there's more than just the general air of depression to guide us. We can identify the trends over a period of three to five years. Are the service numbers going up or down on average? Compare like-with-like and pick out several ordinary Sundays and compare the attendance on those Sundays over several years. Find the Easter Sunday numbers and compare them over several years. I visited a church that was seen by outsiders to be struggling, but it reported having a regular congregation of 25 to 30. While waiting for an after-service meeting I read the service record book and could see that on both ordinary Sundays and Easter over five years the average numbers had gone down by two each year. So, although the church was still functioning, albeit stretched to maintain all its commitments and repair the building, it was clear that continuing on the same journey it would before long have fewer than 20 members and could no longer function realistically as a parish church. It had already reached the stage when the diocese was unwilling to place a paid member of the clergy there.

Review the donations, especially the committed contributions in stewardship programmes. Christians are notorious for putting their money where their hearts are and they will give sacrificially. If committed giving is shrinking or limited to a very small proportion of the members, it is likely to be a symptom of losing heart in the struggle. A new stewardship campaign may make a difference. A root and branch review of how the church might or could finance itself may relieve the pressure. To review finance along with mission is to engage in two key elements of church regeneration.

Many of our churches that struggle to make ends meet, in mission, ministry and money, are actually caring for repair-hungry heritage buildings. A small congregation may be struggling to maintain a cathedral-size building on behalf of their neighbourhood, and for many with Grade I buildings, it is on behalf of the nation, as these are of national significance. Mission and money and buildings go together, and nearly all plans to regenerate the church in its mission, at the same time as making financial sense, must impact on the way we use our buildings and often will involve some adaptation or alteration to them.

Why have we got into this situation, with so many of our churches struggling against the tide? The Church of England has 16,000 parish churches, of which 4,500 are Grade I listed (see information on page 16). This represents 45 per cent of the Grade I buildings in England, and their maintenance should be the responsibility not simply of the 2 per cent who go to church each week but the wider communities who wish the church to continue in general use. In the big picture, outside funders at present contribute perhaps 40 per cent of the £100 million spent on heritage churches each year; the rest comes from the efforts and pockets of churchgoers who maintain these public buildings for and on behalf of everyone.

A key way to change, through the re-engagement of the church with its neighbourhood, can be the route to a new sense of ownership of the church by those who live and work locally, so enabling the individual church to spread the responsibility for a heritage building further into the community for whom it was built.

There are many factors that over years have separated churches from their targeted communities or parishes. For some it's a question of centuries of change, for others a question of decades. A look at some of those factors may enable us to make some changes that might reverse decline; for some we may discover that the change is irreversible and that any regenerated future will have to take up a significantly new identity and direction.

Mission dislocation

Many of the factors identified here are summarized in the phrase 'mission dislocation'. For some, it happened that the church continued to do what it always did while the world changed around them, until one day the people looked around and there was a gulf between the church and its parish. Yet others have taken a determined route that set them against local people and even other church people and their natural supporters and created a divide that has resulted in the drastic decline of the church.

Mission dislocation is evident in:

1 People

Some churches have a long-term pattern of incompetence in their staff and even their volunteers, such as churchwardens. It's as if, having become embarrassed by their own weaknesses, they appoint or elect people who won't show up the inherent problems. A weak leader may promote or encourage the appointment of weak people as 'this is safe'. Sometimes weak clergy leaders are unable to make a move to another church and they stay long beyond what is healthy for their own ministry and the mission of the church. The most helpful route for such churches is the appointment of a strong leader in the next member of the clergy who will be determined to change the culture of weakness and ineffectiveness.

For some churches the ordination of women to the priesthood led to successive traumas, as priests and members of the congregation left for other denominations. The conflict involved dispirited and traumatized everyone. What remains is a rump of what was once a strong mission-and-ministry-focused parish that now has little heart for its mission. Regeneration will have to involve a renewed sense of God, as well as renewed mission and local engagement.

2 Place

Not far from where I grew up is a church in a field and the nearest houses are in a tiny hamlet maybe half a mile away. Between the church and the houses are fields and farms and a busy A-road. This medieval church was once the heart of village life but the centuries of change saw the people go elsewhere. The move is not always so distant, but churches that have become geographically, socially and psychologically removed from their neighbourhoods have different regeneration challenges. In Chapter 7 there is an examination of the church's location; of course the building cannot be moved, but we can examine the context for ways in which people might re-engage with a public building to meet contemporary needs. Some function may be added to the use of the building that will bring in local people. Concerts are drawing people to many church settings for the acoustic qualities and the general ambience. One church I heard about had a pub just across the road where interval drinks were purchased and to which the audience retreated at the end. Concerts cannot be the main element of regeneration if finance is an issue, but may lead to some openings, from lettings for rehearsal and recording to Saturday music school for children.

Where the church has become geographically dislocated we are challenged to find ways to draw local people in through the doors by recognizing the social and cultural realities. Engagement in activity in the church creates familiarity and a sense of ownership.

3 Skills

Many parishes today are run by lone clergy or by clergy shared among several parishes. Clergy training has not changed as fast as the settings in which they need to work, and church members' expectations of their clergy have often not adapted to the new reality of limited clergy time. A church that in the 1960s had a vicar and several curates may now have a vicar who cares for another parish down the road, no curates and possibly a non-stipendiary colleague who has a full-time job elsewhere.

The intense financial and building challenges, the engagement in partnerships with state and charity partners, running and managing community projects, or concert venues, or steering through major fundraising campaigns and construction programmes are all outside the professional training of clergy, and though some have the skills already, others would need training to tackle such issues well. The resultant success rate may be low and churches end up with dilapidated community facilities that are a drain on resources, that is time and money, without really achieving any of their mission targets.

Effective regeneration requires a good balance of professional skills, well-prepared and well-trained teams of clergy, staff and volunteers. Ultimately our national leaders should address the training agenda, but in the meantime we can and must address it at the local level by finding a way to access the development training offered to and by people like us who are engaged in local regeneration: training such as that offered by courses in the charity sector from Councils for the Voluntary Sector, Directory of Social Change and local authority community development departments. New networks such as Faith-based Regeneration Network are adding new perspectives and opportunities to meet like-minded people of faith.

4 Facilities

A relatively small number of people nationally are going to church regularly; I suspect that the majority of the 70 per cent who responded positively in the 2001 census on attending a church may well have attended a wedding. To those who do, the facilities we offer may seem inappropriate and even antiquated.

Many outsiders enjoy the architectural splendour as a backdrop to their activity, but require an acceptable level of lighting (that's adaptable for different uses) and heating. Older church members may remember churches in their childhood when there was no heating, but people will not turn out from their well-heated homes for a church service or concert where they have to wear all their outdoor clothes and still shiver. People also require a clean and well-cared-for toilet that is accessible to disabled people – quality not quantity of toilets matters; most church toilets seem to have poor floor and wall finishes that retain dirt and smells even if they are cleaned regularly. A servery is often needed so refreshments can be served. Many churches have old domestic-style kitchen fittings that have begun to crumble and cannot be thoroughly cleaned, where a servery with stainless steel fittings would be hygienic and serviceable.

A church's regeneration strategy should include bringing all facilities up to acceptable standards and include financial planning that covers a maintenance and upgrading budget to keep them that way.

5 Finances

It is just a couple of decades since Anglican churches could depend on the endowment income through the Church Commissioners to cover the main costs of church life and mission. The change has been at least traumatic, and for some almost impossible. Now the church and its mission have to be maintained by the congregation, and stewardship has taken a high profile. The regular weekly committed donations from church members may nationally add up to something in excess of £400 million but for each individual church that's an average of only £25,000 to pay for everything, and ends do not meet. The development of additional income by more entrepreneurial means is outside the experience of most clergy (though the idea of being an entrepreneur can be captivating), and church councils are set up to maintain the religious life of the church, not to run businesses. There are ways to extend mission while becoming more financially sound, and the preparation of a robust financial plan that incorporates the effective generation of income from assets is a key step for the church council.

Sustainable regeneration of the church will require new training about finance in order to overcome the dislocation of financial expectation by planning effectively for the future. We will not find financial viability and stability unless we plan for it.

6 Building

There is often a profound dislocation between local neighbourhoods and church buildings. The building is often over-
large, not understood, and perceived as irrelevant. Recent
generations of children have not engaged in the history, stories
and traditions of their locality; few have visited a church
where the story is unfolded for them and their own links to
the church's heritage opened up for them.

The preparation of programmes and publications, open
days and welcome events will be essential for new dimensions
of local 'ownership'. We can no longer open the doors and
expect people to know what they are looking at and where
it fits into their life experiences. Efforts to create stepping-
stones, between the complete outsider and engagement in a
building that belongs to everyone, will have to be planned and
activated.

Summary

Dislocation is a serious challenge that cannot be addressed by
churches trying to go back to where they were. The evidence
of a struggling church, one that has started on the slippery
slope of decline, may be in the people, financial problems, a
difficult location, unattainable repair challenges or just sheer
unsuitability for the present job, or various combinations of
all five.

A regeneration strategy for churches, particularly in the
Church of England where each is an independently functioning body, will have to focus on those individual churches.
The roles of dioceses and senior staff may be most effective
in comprehensively understanding, and offering appropriate
professional support and advice. Training in planning, management and development could and perhaps should be available to both clergy and lay leaders.

3

Can We Turn the Corner? Do We Want To?

Having identified signs of failure and ineffectiveness, can any particular church or building be made to deliver the purpose and aims of its members, to regenerate the church to re-engage with the neighbourhood, whether urban or rural? Will the church change its worship life to make openings for new people and methods of helping them join in activity that is often alien to them? Does the church have the strength to make the change to engage with and develop avenues of mutual support with local people of all faiths and none? Does it have the strength and determination to engage in activity that benefits local people who are in need?

Mission and ministry can be delivered through programmes which need new skills and outside funding. The agenda and demand for change must come from inside the church, and often dramatic change requires fresh leadership: either present people making significant change through training, or adding new staff with new skills – they don't all have to be clergy. How do you wish to express the *church's* (that is the church's not just the vicar's) sense of mission and ministry in new programmes of activity that are wanted and needed by local people?

It is important to consider together the age, profile, skills and competences of staff and key members. Do they want to change, and do they know how to change?

Changing the culture of the church to becoming outward-looking, open to local opportunities, requires changes at leadership level, and the leaders should be prepared to require change at all levels of the organization, leading by example. Sometimes the leader needs to change before change can get under way!

Change and emotions

The Church of England and other major denominations have in recent decades been severely affected by changes in the cost of staff, and the changes in pension laws have brought many notable churches to a parlous financial state. Eventually in another couple of decades the pension situation will recover itself, and more money will be available from sources such as the Church Commissioners, but the challenge is at its height now. Despite the Church of England being the recipient collectively of over £400 million per annum made up from weekly donations, this pans out to only £25,000 for each of its 16,000 churches, and is clearly insufficient to pay for both buildings and religious activity.

The Church of England has:

- 4,200 Grade I or A churches, representing 45 per cent of all Grade I or A buildings
- 4,200 Grade II* churches, representing 20 per cent of all Grade II* buildings.
- 3,800 Grade II or C churches.
- 4,000 unlisted.[2]

That is 16,200 churches, and the repair bill is estimated at £100 million per annum, with approximately 60 per cent of that sum coming from the efforts of church members. The remaining 40 per cent comes from outside funders.

Locally focused parish churches have been built and maintained, cared for and often loved by a multitude of supporters over decades of minor ups and downs. They have taken on a

---

2 Trevor Cooper, *How Do We Keep Our Parish Churches?* The Ecclesiological Society, 2004.

life together. Now faced with the realization that their best efforts in the direction in which they are going are insufficient for them to retain their treasured buildings is traumatic in many ways.

Recent national reports such as *Building Faith in our Future*, from the Church Heritage Forum, identify not just the financial situation but the disengagement of many churches from their neighbourhood and their natural and potential catchment areas as causes of problems. Perhaps the church was orphaned by cultural and societal changes in the twentieth century; or perhaps it makes choices to live in the past and so attracts people who look to the past for stability and security; the very people who are least able to cope with making dramatic change in order to survive.

Insofar as the church has become inward-looking and self-serving, it has separated itself from the many people who historically may not have been active church members but would have counted themselves as supporters of its role in local social cohesion and local sense of goodwill. There are many who might once have expected to use the church for rites of passage, for whom that is now an alien thought. The solution to many of the current challenges is for the local church to focus actively on re-engaging with its neighbourhood.

Re-engagement with the locality may reconnect the local church with new opportunities to establish the activity and thereby the income that makes it sustainable. Of course, that hinterland of interests, cultures and activities has changed dramatically in the past few decades. For rural communities there may well be many commuters or people without local loyalty who want to live the rural idyll while their children are young, yet whose work and social focus is elsewhere. Urban localities may be numerically dominated by people of other faiths. High-rise buildings from past decades surround, dwarf and diminish fine Grade I urban churches and leave them isolated and misunderstood. Industrial areas where the industry has closed or moved away are bereft of energy, peopled by the disabled and pensioners, people who seem already to have lost the battle for productive life in times of change. Remarkably, the spirit of the church seems often to reflect the spirit of the neighbourhood – even while it has become separated. Too often congregations seem to try to do harder what they were already doing, without realizing that their present strategy got them into this hole, and that digging harder will only take them deeper.

Change has to happen inside the church if re-engagement is going to be possible. Emotional and psychological barriers to development and progress may exist, and opening up new ways of thinking and behaving may be the first step. For example:

- Letting more and new people 'feel' they own the building and allowing this to impact on the way the building is used;
- Accepting change to long-standing patterns and habits in building maintenance and management;
- Accepting that change will permeate the church's life on every front, even having an impact on the way the church engages in its religious activity.

Change that aims to re-engage with local neighbourhoods can be set out and planned in a managed way, that is by looking at all the resources available – people, building, finance – and re-allocating them according to a new purpose. Buildings and money are neutral regarding change, as they are secondary, and not the reason why change is happening. People are organic and experience trauma when change happens, even when that change is chosen or inevitable!

It might be suggested that the vicar should do the work of making regeneration happen in a change of job description for the sake of productivity. But does s/he have both the motivation and the skills? And the people with whom s/he was doing her/his previous pastoral and liturgical activity may well be unhappy, that is unless they own and are passionate about the change.

How to change

To take the ailing or moribund congregation in a new direction in order to deal with an ailing building will need more than management. It will take new leadership. Either the old leader with new energy and direction or – very often – new leaders!

That new leader or group of leaders will face several key tasks:

1 Changing the culture (has to be done from the top down and by more than one person).
2 Owning and engaging with the congregation's negative feelings, the sense of loss, violation, anger, grief. The decreasing church congregation nearly always has built up a network of interdependent emotional crutches to keep them on their downward-spiralling journey.
3 Changing the sense of direction, even when communicating hope, will in fact generate fear in a group that has probably stayed in a failing church for reasons that include disliking change and wanting the old ways. For these people all change is traumatic. They don't like adventures or challenges. However, developing a culture of change, challenge and adventure will be attractive to people who previously did not want to be drawn into the stability model of the church – they may like the new, more entrepreneurial one.
4 Managing change in ways that do not further jeopardize the stability of the church, that is its finances and its ability to meet its present commitments out of current resources. Growing too fast can kill an organization just as readily as inactivity. But the change required for a comfortable transition in resources can easily be used to negotiate the transition that people need emotionally. A hasty transition that violates people emotionally will lose the engagement and commitment that have maintained the church to date.

Summary

Decide whether the church not only has the potential for change, but also the will and determination to change.

Consider whether new clerical and lay leadership needs to be developed or brought in, or whether the skills are in place.

4

Models of Change

Remarkably, when the odds are considered, there are many models of regeneration and new life in churches up and down the country. Each of these has addressed the worship life of the church alongside new initiatives in mission and ministry. Going out to meet and work with local residents has been the locus of new friendships and new interest in the core activity of the church; growth has happened on all fronts.

The everyday church

In the late 1980s, a church in London welcomed their new vicar. He was well known to them as the curate of the church down the road. While one church languished in a numerical and mission doldrums, the neighbouring church was dramatically increasing its numbers, success was breeding success with large multi-ethnic congregations every Sunday and huge numbers for Festivals.

The new vicar did not want to detract from the neighbours. Whatever success came to the church he was happy to work on that success being something that did not depend on failure down the road and his aim was to enable the church through re-engaging with its neighbourhood to become an everyday church.

A large and beautiful Grade II* church opens off one of the main traffic routes into London and is surrounded by deteriorating Victorian and Edwardian housing and 'mansion' buildings divided into small flats by the local authority. It is an area of poverty and social transition.

The church began, after an assessment of all its resources and assets, by productively disposing of the semi-derelict church hall; it was leased to a co-operative. The lease gave a discounted rent to the co-operative for fifteen years, in return for which the tenants would do all the repairs and upgrading, so that a commercial rent would appropriately apply after the fifteen years.

Within the church itself the nave was opened up for meetings and bookings by local groups. A side entrance foyer became a meeting room booked by smaller groups. The large gallery was converted to office space housing the building administrator and the offices of the youth workers and employment project staff.

Under the gallery volunteers developed a charity shop well used by local people. As the years passed and the building became more than packed with daily activity a small extension was added to house a café/restaurant serving local residents and workers with healthy food.

The 'business' strategy of this multi-faceted endeavour was simple; each element or department had to be financially self-sufficient and pay its share of the costs of using the building, as well as its own running costs. Some projects were clearly money earners while offering, for example, work opportunities and training in the café to local people, but this let no-one off the hook: each one had to be viable. The sum total is a church intimately involved in the warp and weft of the social and cultural fabric of its neighbourhood, with a new-found financial sustainability and a powerfully expressed engagement in outreach.

'Open the doors' church

St Michael's Church is located almost at the heart of one of London's busiest attractions, the markets and street culture bringing in more than 1 million people each week. But the church had lost its way. Despite being a Grade II* church it was desperately in need of repair and was ten years ago the only London church named on English Heritage's register of buildings-at-risk.[3]

And the congregation was as depressed as the building. Only ten people remained on the electoral roll and they had stopped using the main door; they abandoned the nave to accumulating rubbish and worshipped in the chancel. The parish room was falling down, the surrounding land diminished as the supermarket built next door took land that wasn't theirs (they have now paid for it!) and the area became waterlogged when the adjacent construction site damaged the drains. If that wasn't enough, the church is below street level and when a water main burst in the local high street the nave became a 'swimming pool'.

The vision of the new vicar who arrived ten years ago may be summarized as 'Open the doors and the people will come in!'

Since the main door stands open almost every day, with one of London's biggest supermarkets next door and busy bus stops on the pavement beneath the west window, the people have flocked in. For the first few years the average congregation doubled each year and is still increasing. Easter now has an attendance of 150. Volunteers, Christmas card stalls, local exhibitions and school events keep the main doors open, and the building is well known as the largest community meeting space in the town.

More recently funds have been raised to locate community project staff in the old and repaired parish room. This enables increased engagements in the issues that impact on the lives of local people. Repairs to the structure of the building have begun.

The change of leadership that opened up a change of culture and renewed mission and ministry suited to the church and location has been the means of regeneration.

---

3 Not many working churches are placed on the list, except in *extremis*, as the continuing congregation may feel that they are receiving one more stamp of failure when they really need encouragement to build themselves up.

Rural churches

From 1998 to 2001 the Rural Churches in Community Service programme was funded by the Millennium Commission to facilitate the development of community projects in church buildings.[4]

A village of 500 people, close to the Grand Union Canal with a medieval church that is listed Grade I, converted a room in the church's north aisle to accommodate a kitchen, a disabled-accessible toilet and a new meeting room above. A thirteenth-century doorway was reopened to give level access for disabled people. The church now accommodates social activities, concerts and other cultural events for residents, visitors and those from other villages, and regular events for children, parents with toddlers, and pensioners. The new opportunity has provided a creative partnership with the local school, and church services have had increased congregations.

A village of 300 people, with a chapel and pub its only other public buildings, has a Grade I fifteenth-century church. The project to create new facilities provided kitchen and toilet in the base of the tower, a small meeting room, disabled access throughout the building and improvement to make the nave more flexible in its use. Nowadays 120 people each month use the church for social events, meetings, concerts, craft classes, education and training and tourist activities.

A village of 850 with a Celtic chapel, a nuclear power station, the remains of a Roman fort and a marina has as many as 36,000 visitors each year. The Grade II* listed church has a

---

4 Susan Rowe, *A Review of the Rural Churches in Community Service Programme*, February 2004.

chancel from the thirteenth century. The regeneration project provided a carpeted entrance, kitchenette and disabled-accessible toilet and improved meeting space. Since opening, the church has welcomed visitors, and used ground-floor meeting space for elderly and disabled people, social clubs, study groups for visitors and local exhibitions.

The report by Susan Rowe is an inspiring read as so many relatively small projects have engaged their communities in partnership in new projects that have provided facilities for all sorts of local people and visitors. Many projects required less than £100,000, which money from the Millennium Commission matched with local fundraising was able to provide.

The marketplace church

Located in the city centre, one urban church funds its many community activities out of income derived from an entrepreneurial package of activities. The market in the church courtyard provides sufficient money to employ a staff of vergers who keep the church open and safe every day. Endless streams of tourists pour in, and along with them come a significant number of dysfunctional people, homeless, drug and alcohol dependent, or with mental health problems. To meet the need of the latter the church has a caravan alongside the market providing drop-in advice and support. But that doesn't pay the bills for the church's maintenance, so in addition the meeting rooms used by the church for a variety of social and pastoral activities in evenings and at weekends are let out to a number of groups, commercial and community. The daily programme of evening concerts and lunchtime recitals is self-funding, the charges for using the church nave cover the cost of hiring staff to organize and maintain the programme. On average around 1,000 people each day visit the market and the church, attend services, enjoy concerts and recitals or use the church meeting rooms.

There is a multitude of inspiring examples. Before a church sets out on its own regeneration strategy it is worth enquiring about other people's successes and failures and taking a church group on visits. Ask those visited about what they appreciate about the change and what they would have done differently if they had another chance. Ask church members to reflect on what they liked and disliked about the changes they saw and why. Their views will help inform the changes your church makes.

Summary

There are many models for regenerating churches; yours will be different from all the others. The successful models are those that prepared well for their locations and for the financial and staffing realities of their setting.

The key for each regenerated church was in discovering ways to engage with the needs of local people while developing new sources of income from existing assets.

5

Create the Church's Development Team

To establish regeneration through re-engagement with the local community as the strategy for the future, it is advisable to create a small team that includes several key roles. Many small churches, some in villages of a few hundred people, undertake regeneration programmes of greater or lesser magnitude. For these churches a team such as that listed below is a dream beyond imagining. However, this list of roles may enable two or three people to consider how each of the functions will be achieved among them, what skills are missing and how they can compensate for the latter. Churches in supportive communities have also co-opted local residents with appropriate skills to work with them.

The targets of the team

- To identify possible changes that are needed.
- To discover common ground and common objectives with outside agencies and individuals.
- To get the view of stakeholders, including local residents, along with their ideas, interests and concerns.
- To engage with the interests of outside agencies and develop mutual concerns and possible ways forward for neighbourhood regeneration.
- To make connections, exploring the possibility of mutually beneficial outcomes.
- To explore potential funding sources and contributions.

The make-up of the team

The team should include a variety of skills and roles. Someone may represent more than one function in the team, and leadership can and probably should rest with different people at different times; this is not necessarily in a formal way, but at the point of their strengths several people will effectively lead from time to time. Do consider this carefully, ensuring that you are very honest about the real skills of the vicar. Anyone who is a priest normally commands the respect of the people and has a leadership function in the congregation and church council, but that does not mean they are multi-skilled or able to do everything. Consider your vicar in a role on the team that plays to their strengths, not the ones they would like to have or you would like them to have.

Chairperson

This is someone who can find the way forward, keeping everyone steady while

- ensuring everyone in the team has a say
- ensuring every issue is fully explored and all perceptions, thoughts and feelings are on the table (so resentments don't build up)
- empathising with all viewpoints on the team and enabling people with differences to work together
- being a mediator
- summarizing and then moving things forward.

Champion

The champion is someone with connections who can advance the project. The champion may have a wide social or business circle of contacts and can represent the project in various forums. When dealing with large organizations and businesses it is incredibly helpful to have a champion perceived as a peer who 'speaks their language' and can drop in an affirming word outside the church from time to time.

The champion is determined to make the project happen and will not give up when there are problems. On the team, the champion may be able to sort out internal problems and drive forward.

Administrator

The administrator will be responsible for the minutes of meetings and much more. This person will be systematic, keep records and ensure that everyone has the information they need. Expect the administrator also to want to keep order as the project proceeds.

Ankle-biter

There is breed of small dog called an Ormskirk Heeler that was originally bred to keep cows in order by nipping at their heels. The ankle-biter is the person who keeps everyone to their commitments. Expect this person to have a strong sense of time and priorities and to focus on what needs to happen next (the Critical Path). The ankle-biter can be expected to embarrass people into doing the things that they said they would do.

Problem-solver

Here is/are the person/s (your team may have more than one problem-solver) who do/es the work! Include someone who does whatever is needed to get the project done, from problems in construction to organizing a reception. They will be passionate about finding solutions. This person will already be busy but they always will be! The problem-solver may lead volunteers in key activities like getting out a mailing, or setting up an event. In the business world the problem-solver would be the business manager and Number 2 to whoever is seen as the 'boss'.

Public relations and communication

Have someone on the team with skills in communication. They will ensure that people outside the church know about the project and are seeing it in a good light. This person will understand how to present the church to outsiders in the language of those outsiders. Ask this person to work on a communication programme so that newsletters or articles are produced as necessary for the local community to know about and engage with the church.

Leadership

Any member of the team may be the leader, and it will vary as the project progresses. A good leader lets others take the lead at times, and this is a fix-it function that keeps the team going.

The method of the team

Outline ways of tackling elements of the external exploration, and set up expectations of the written material each team member will produce. (Set a level playing-field so that styles of reporting don't skew or control the way the project goes forward.) Understand what commitment each person can/ cannot make on behalf of everyone – this is an exploration stage so, when meeting with an outside agency, a good ending may be: 'I would like to come back to you on this as it seems a really good potential way to develop.' The input of the team and ultimately of the church council will be needed before a firm commitment can be made.

Look over all the elements of Cycle One and work out how the team is going to break the work down into tasks and allocate these tasks to individuals. Set timescales for achieving the tasks and a programme indicating when the team expects the tasks to be completed. Set a schedule of team meetings to allow for updates before all the work is complete.

Create the Church's Development Team

Summary

The make-up of the team is determined by the kinds of tasks that will need to be achieved.

The roles on the team are defined not by status but by skills. Leadership may come at different times from every member of the team.

Churches without enough people to fill the roles could look outside the church membership.

Small churches such as rural churches may have only one or two people able to work on the regeneration project. They should work within their skills while being prepared to ask for help or to try new things as these arise. Overall a tiny church will be far less able to tackle a big project and may be advised to start small and grow as more resources become available over the years.

Part 2

The Development Cycle

6

Using the Development Cycle to Set Up the Church's Route to Regeneration

I received this communication from one vicar. 'Our church wants to create some community facilities so I phoned the archdeacon who told me to talk to our architect and get plans and then get back to him and the Diocesan Advisory Committee for permission. I am sure there's a lot more to it, can you help?' There is a lot more to it, and creating a systematic pathway through the many complex issues around the regeneration of a church in its engagement with its neighbours has been the solution.

Over the two decades during which I have been working with churches in the process of regeneration and renewal it has become very clear that there is a multitude of considerations and issues that bear down upon such attempts. Most of the related authorities would wish to preserve the building in its present use but their role is not to generate creativity but rather the exercise of controls to prevent misuse or destructive projects; it is not always obvious how the regeneration project is going to turn out, and authorities hesitate. Regeneration initiatives are risky, and knowing that there is both a systematic approach that reduces risk and that individual churches are using it, can be reassuring. At the same time various agencies are urging churches to become productive community buildings serving their neighbourhoods but fail to understand how to meet the ongoing needs of the church congregation, among whom is the will to develop and reach out. Then there are church members and clergy who have seen a great idea elsewhere and want to bring it here. 'St So-and-so had a nursery (read also café, homeless project, mother and toddler group) and it was great. That's what we should do.'

Think of the set of Cycles that follow as being a tool. It's yours to adapt and use. Some people will take the outline and run with it, fitting their own perspective and experience into its framework and use it therefore as a system for creating order in a chaotic and often bewildering process. Others will take the tool and work more freely with the detailed descriptive material that stems from the experience and learning of many churches that have grappled with the issues of regeneration.

The process is, like a running track, a circuit around which we progress three times. The purpose of each turn is different, though many of the issues visited or people talked to will be the same. The relationships and tasks involved will progress significantly with each turn. Why not complete it in one turn? Simply, you start with an internal idea of what the church wants but can't tell whether it is going to work in your neighbourhood until you have met with others in the neighbourhood who also are looking at its needs, so the narrowing of options only becomes clear after consultation in the neighbourhood. Once the church has its Preferred Option at the end of Cycle One, the plan needs to be both tested for financial viability and in other ways internally but also developed externally with people who will become partners and supporters. People who may become tenants in the church will require dedicated time building up a relationship that is expressed in a lease or letting agreement and the realities of letting rates they can accommodate. On the third lap the development work, consolidated into a 'business' plan, ensures that all the i's are dotted and all the t's crossed for a viable long-term development.

The first circuit is *exploration of possibilities*, resulting in the first draft of the strategy.

The second circuit is *detailed negotiation and consolidation*, ensuring that the way the church intends to go is workable with the potential partners they have discovered (including potential funding partners) and within the limitations of the church's resources and values.

The third circuit is *comprehensive planning and legal agreements*, with assurance that the strategy is well supported and various sectors of the local community are actively engaged and committed to the plan.

The purpose of the entire process is:

1 To re-engage with the church neighbourhood.
2 To reach out in ministry through including local people in a variety of activities that are of benefit to our neighbourhood, residents and workers.[5]
3 To develop in ways that renew or increase the church's financial viability and sustainability.

The process as laid out and followed in this book involves report-making and reporting to key people that require the team to revisit the church's purposes at regular intervals, ensuring that the activity itself doesn't drift too far from the original aims. The Development Cycle covers many possibilities, some of which may not appear applicable to your situation. There is no great need to follow it slavishly; instead tackle everything that seems relevant and important: you can come back to items that only later prove to be important. I would recommend that all the internal elements are completed, and

---

5 In my experience, once people are coming and going in the church building meeting friendship and welcome, evangelism happens quite naturally with people attending church out of curiosity or at times of distress without feeling it too strange or uncomfortable. But we have to be ready with a welcome and support.

especially that clear reports are made available to church members and interested outside bodies. It is a great disadvantage if the key elements and supportive information are held in the minds of two or three people and not open to and inclusive of everyone else.

7

Cycle One:
Exploring the Possibilities

With each turn of the Development Cycle there are three key phases: first, internal planning and development; second, external work with all kinds of agencies and individuals who are significant to the effectiveness of the final plan; and third, an internal gathering of that learning into a report.

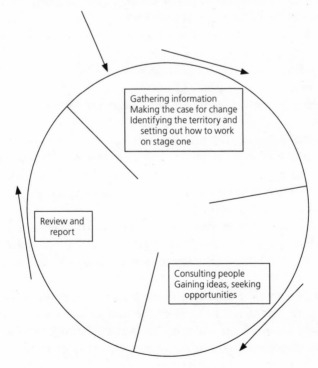

Gathering information
Making the case for change
Identifying the territory and
   setting out how to work
   on stage one

Review and
report

Consulting people
Gaining ideas, seeking
opportunities

First, a small working group (or even the vicar and church-wardens) may be the core of getting this started. But when the tasks are understood, this working group is encouraged to build a small team of people with a variety of skills who can most ably carry this forward. See page 27.

Beginning the process

Bringing a body of people along on a strategy that will change the life of the church requires effective and encompassing ownership. The change will be a cause of broken relationships, conflict and argument if foundations are not laid before new ideas come into play.

First, recognize the unproductive rut or the downward slide. Review the church attendance records over five years and produce a summary of what has happened. Review the church finances and summarize the situation carefully: Is the income keeping level in real terms with the demands of running the church? Again, five years is a good review period. What other activities has the church run over the past five years? Have these increased or decreased? How many people have benefited each year? Questions such as these will tell the church whether change has to be made for the sake of survival.

If these issues are not pressing, the church still may want to make major changes because of its vision for the church and neighbourhood. Still, the groundwork will have to be in place for the church members to accept that change is necessary for discipleship and growth.

When the church community has accepted the reality of the situation and is agreeable if not wholehearted about change, then the search for a strategy for regeneration can get under way.

It is worthwhile spending time, perhaps on an away-day, asking church members to voice the important values of the church's life. For some churches the sense of a busy extended family may be dominant, for others the sense of order and ritual may predominate. It is important to identify where the sense of the presence of God is recognized. Does the church hold a great sense of the numinous, encouraging both Christian and non-Christian to realize that this is sacred space? What else is important and valued? Hold on to these reflections as regeneration is pursued, for the spiritual life of each member in their relationship to God is a lot of what church is about. As we enable people to find a place to encounter God, it is important that we then help to maintain that sense of place. Often people change as they get older, often they change as they meet new and enriching experiences, and so our change for regeneration should proceed at a pace and with a programme that enriches the spiritual journeys of members and does not turn them away.

Summary

Until everyone accepts that change is essential to the church's life and ministry, plans once made will continue to be faced with internal opposition.

Consider every element of the life of the church and how change might impact upon it.

Be sure that preparation for change is based on the church's highest concerns and values: for worship and mission.

Gather information

Resources needed to continue present work

Many of us are so familiar with the ordinary patterns of use of our building that we are no longer aware of whether we are using it efficiently or effectively for our church activity.

Walk around every part of the church, hall and other property and see how every space is used. If possible make notes on a ground plan (the inspecting architect may be able to send a copy or make a rough sketch) showing how often the space is used: for how many hours by how many people in what group.

The schedule will show how much of the space is fully used for the church's own religious activity: worship, pastoral care, meetings and events. Is space being kept vacant because of aspects that are inconvenient; is the only easy route to the church office via the nave, therefore the nave never has alternative use? It may be possible at a later stage in development to ask the architect for a design solution to the access issues that keep spaces empty. Don't get tempted to make decisions such as 'No one would want to use the nave for anything other than church services because of the pews.' In fact, many churches with pews in place hold non-church functions, and in many churches permission will be given for removing some or all of the pews; for now, consider building space only as space.

Now it is possible to assess how much vacant space there is that is relatively unused. But do bear in mind that the church's plans for mission and outreach may require some more meeting space; these needs should also be quantified.

Consider the church's plans for evangelism and church groups. Do these plans involve more use of space? If they do, add those planned uses to the schedule.

Then, consider how well the spaces that are occupied by the church are suited to contemporary use. Is there sufficient security protection for clergy and other staff in the building (remember the susceptibility to attack)? Is there a meeting room with a change of floor level in the middle because it was once a side chapel? Are there areas not reached by the heating, access doors that are unopenable, areas that are not suitably lit? Are there areas or rooms filled with items stored in case they might one day be useful? Even storage for jumble sales can be cleared out after each sale and sent to a charity shop so valuable rooms can be put to active use.

Consider the nave and chancel: are they ordered for contemporary worship? Theology in the last half-century has resulted in significant change in liturgical patterns, and to accommodate the many people in your neighbourhood who might visit or attend a regenerated and attractive church, is your liturgical space suited to people being able to see, hear and engage actively in what is going on?

If it is a struggle to assess the spaces, try the exercise: 'If you moved across the road and built a brand-new church what would you take with you?' Work in small groups and report back with plans, maps or diagrams. This will highlight what the church values and identifies, what members like least or find least helpful and useful.

In addition, the team might consider now whether the welcome and introduction that people are given when they arrive at the church helps them to feel included. In addition to service sheets and books which are familiar to the congregation, how would the stranger to churchgoing know what is happening and why? Does the congregation look out for people who are bemused or bewildered and sit alongside them to help them know what is going on? If someone's first church visit is to a Eucharist, how will they know its purpose and whether to do what everyone else does – should they or shouldn't they?

Worship

At the end of this review the team should have a schedule of worship services, the numbers who on average attend, with a note of the maximum numbers, and any special additional factors that come into play, such as the need to have refreshments at the end of some services.

Assess also the amount of time being spent by clergy, staff and volunteers on the work they currently undertake. Use this as a method of determining whether the church has surplus resources that can be reallocated to new projects in the church's regeneration, maybe to run a new activity group but perhaps more often to provide a member of a steering group or management committee.

Mission

In light of the church's mission plan, make a clear note of new activity: when, for whom, for how many people and in what space that activity will take place and whose skills and time are required to lead it. If the vicar is leading the group, does the activity group need a deputy in case s/he is needed for, for example, a funeral?

Office

Does the church administration and management take place in the church building? Is the office adequate?

Is there adequate and suitable space for the vicar/priest to meet with individuals in need? Many clergy now prefer to bring such functions into the church for safety reasons where other people are nearby.

Consider as a summary the spaces that are available in the building and the time that individuals have or could have for new activity.

Look back at the strengths and weaknesses chart and add any useful additional information. It doesn't matter if it gets rather long, you can précis it later.

Report: prepare a one-page summary using bullet points of the resources the church's activities require (both those existing and those that are desirable). Indicate separately the space required, the people and skills required and the finance required, both existing and new. Accompany this with a schedule of current use that can also indicate the times of inactivity that are available for additional use or activity.

Summary

Understand the church's present worship, mission and outreach to ensure that there are sufficient resources to maintain and increase these in a growing church.

Assess staff, building and finance requirements for the continuing life and ministry of the church.

The church and other building assets

Churches are commonly asset rich and cash poor. They may even be closed down because of financial pressures at the same time as owning extremely valuable assets in their buildings and land. This audit is designed to help a church understand the capital value of its assets and raise questions and ideas about how those capital assets might contribute considerably to relieving the cash or revenue pressure.

Unused space has a potential income value if a suitable use can be found from the commercial or community sectors. Churches have typically let out their surplus space at ridiculously low levels. The result has been that there is never enough money to keep the quality of those building spaces up to a reasonable standard for regular use. Almost every church hall I visit falls into this category, and even new church hall spaces are being let out at less than cost. (Cost can be calculated from adding direct administrative costs, all utilities, insurance, repair and an accrual for major repairs.)

Since the building space (hall and church) is an asset of the church not needed (all the time) for the church's religious purposes, it is considered by Charity Law an asset to be invested to make a return to the charity for its religious objectives. It is like putting money in a bank account and using the interest as regular cash income. Consider the church hall an endowment, usable by the church as it requires, but earning income for the church when it is surplus to church demand.

Many church halls, basements and crypts house activities that 'have always been there' and the rent never rose and concessions have crept in to the detriment of the church itself.

One church had a social club, established many decades before as an outreach to local people, in its basement. The social need for a gathering place for families with a church affiliation or connection had long since gone, and for the past few decades the social club had become an alternative pub for people who lived nearby. Cash businesses are always open to corruption, and rumour had it that in its heyday the club had provided good incomes for its officers (who were supposedly volunteers), but now it was down on its luck. The club committee was asking the church to forgo rent for a few months till the Christmas season when things would improve. First, the only way to forgo or delay rent was for the church itself to pay the club's bills (the rent was more nearly a service charge than rent). Clearly these bills did not fall within the religious or mission activities of the church (supplying alcohol is not a charitable activity *and* the club's members were avowedly not interested in church at all and disliked the clergy even coming into the club) but could the church defer the rent – listing the costs as a loan? The vicar and treasurer asked for the club's financial records to identify whether in an average year, and average Christmas season, the club could recoup its position and pay off current and back rent. It quickly became clear that the club had insufficient cashflow projected to even buy its next barrel of beer; even a great Christmas season of drinking could not do more than pay the rent at the time; by spring the club would not only have today's rent debt but a renewed inability to pay. The church decided not to accept a gap in rental payments and recommended to the club's members that they take the decision to close the club and join another social club in the area. Within months the basement was relet to a community group grant-aided by the local authority, so it paid a higher rent and that rent was guaranteed. The church basement still served local people (and many more than before) and now contributed as an asset of the church to its funds for mission.

Commercial values

Through a local chartered surveyor or estate agent, ascertain the potential values of commercial use of the church's surplus building space. This is not completely straightforward as details about location, access, desirability, level of demand all impact on values.

But as an example ask the surveyor to consider:

- An empty room in the tower (great view) for letting as an office.
- A church hall let as office, warehouse or workshop.
- A meeting room let as an office.

The information will probably be given as pounds per square foot or square metre, meaning there will a rental payment of £x for each unit of area for each year.

Adapting building spaces to office or workshop use involves a capital expense essential before such income could be realized. However, a comprehensive business plan (see below, page 166) will enable the church to approach regeneration agencies who are seeking to establish business start-up spaces in the area. Job creation and tackling unemployment is still high on the social agenda.

> The roof space, with the floor appropriately laid, was let as offices in one London church in the early 1990s when office space was cheap and small offices here earned £2,000 each per year. Now a decade later the value has more than doubled and many 2- or 3-person businesses are waiting to take on such spaces.

Consult a housing association; you may have a diocesan housing association or one with local interests. Ask for an assessment of building on church land (not the graveyard but unconsecrated land) such as church hall land, possibly rebuilding the hall with flats above or with housing alongside. Such an arrangement would leave the church with a fully refurbished hall that can be used and let to earn income.

Community values

The real letting value of church halls and community spaces should be ascertained.

Obtain a list of local spaces let to local groups, families and individuals for events, meetings and regular community groups. Lists of lettable community halls are often available from the local authority. Get a list and phone each centre or building and get their letting details, remembering to note the different functions that book the space and at what rates.

For example:

Location	Uses	Price per hour
Town hall	Major events and receptions (up to 200)	
Methodist hall	Local groups like tenants' associations (up to 50)	
Scout hut	Scouts but also exercise classes (up to 30)	
St E's church hall	Nursery every day plus evening groups (up to 100)	
Village hall		
Library		

Now compare the church's own lettable spaces:

Location	Possible daytime use	Possible evening use	Possible weekend use
Nave			
Hall			
Small hall			
Meeting room			

Find the average cost of the space of similar size and capacity in other places. It might be worth dropping local church halls out of this equation as they may well be letting out space at below cost. If the church hall was let regularly at these rates throughout the year, would it earn sufficient to give income over and above running costs and overheads? If the letting income cannot meet the running costs, then another of the options for development may be more desirable. A sample church hall budget and letting rates are included on page 154. They may be helpful in planning a comprehensive budget for comparison.

Selling assets

In making recommendations about the church's assets look extremely carefully at long-term issues before selling property to finance new work. If selling an asset that has the potential to earn income – for example a church hall – ensure that the capital value is not lost. Selling the hall and spending the money on the church roof merely uses up the asset so that when another financial need arises there is neither asset nor money. If the sale value is invested in the bank the church still has the interest earned to spend on essentials, and the capital retains its value and earning potential. If the money is spent on lettable facilities (in the church perhaps after the hall is sold) the capital may retain its investment value as the new facilities may earn income from the capital investment. In the latter case it is less easy to turn that asset back into cash, so this should be borne in mind; but at least in this case the money is still working.

Statement of significance

Before planning change that may affect the church building, it is important to have a much wider sense of the building and its significance historically, architecturally, socially and culturally. It is becoming common for churches to be asked for a statement of significance about their building when applying to the diocesan Advisory Committee for faculty approval. However, it seems that many churches are asking their architect to write such statements. Bear in mind that the architect may be well versed in the architectural significance of the building and maybe even elements of its history, but there is so much the architect will never know. Prepare the statement yourselves and ask the architect to contribute later from her/his perspective.

The significance of the church includes its ongoing story, and regeneration is simply a new page being turned. Consider and write briefly on each of the following:

- The architectural importance, its original design and mission.
- The history of the church and any notable episodes, and add the memories of the church's present oldest members. What

did the church do at the end of the war, on Coronation Day and on other special days? Are there special memories of fellowship and traditions in the past?

- The significance of features of the church that may not be of great architectural merit but are important to current or older members; the stations of the cross may be an example. Regeneration that alters the building should consider this significance as much as that valued by outside agencies. The values, commitment and faith of the members is embodied in this place; they matter as much as anyone, so it is important to keep their values engaged in the future, through the symbols they treasure.
- The significance of the church and its buildings to the neighbouring residents. Do they use the facilities of the hall? Do they know-and-love or know-and-hate the building? Does the church add value to their environment?
- Is the church part of the fabric of the community? When local issues arise that impact positively or negatively on people's lives or environment, is the church part of the network of celebration or campaigning? If it is not, it may be that one element of regeneration is to establish a recognized role for the church at the heart of local community activity.
- Does the church have a cultural role or function in maintaining the social fabric? When a community consultation is needed by a local agency, such as the local authority, is the church a natural place in which to be? Are school or community events naturally held here, or does everyone look elsewhere? Is the church used for concerts, social occasions and rites of passage?

Building repair needs

Make a list of repair needs from the church's quinquennial inspection report. And if the church has buildings not covered by the Quinquennial Inspection system, note their repair needs. If the church has in place a programme for making the repairs, include brief information on the programme. If there is no such programme, then the repair of buildings will become a more significant element of the regeneration project.

Every church is being encouraged by dioceses and the major agencies funding repairs to have an active maintenance programme in place. A good programme will keep up with minor works and prevent most of them becoming major works; if gutters and drains are kept clear and slipped slates replaced, there is much less chance of water leaking into the building and causing rot and other damage.

Using the past five years' records of maintenance, heat and light costs, insurance and other running expenses such as paying for a caretaker, create a sample annual budget for the cost of running each of the church's buildings. Make a second budget, if necessary, of projected costs if the buildings become busy, for example, if they are heated every day and not just at weekends.

These sets of building costs will become crucial to proving the viability of the building regeneration, and any programmes or additional uses that result from the church's renewed mission will need to at least offset such costs.

Report. Allocate perhaps half a page of each of these elements of building asset assessment: repair needs, community values and commercial values. Include the full statement of significance, which may be a couple of pages or more, as this will give a good perspective on building solutions to everyone who needs to read the report.

Summary

The church's building assets may be tools for mission and ministry or sources of income to provide for mission and ministry. If a church is really down on its resources of staff, volunteers, programmes and money, then using the buildings more commercially as a source of finance to pay for church administration, youth and children's workers and other church activities is possible. Other churches may be able to build up the resources they need while letting out surplus building space to community groups at an hourly rate. Both routes can pay for the staff and other resources needed when the church becomes a busy hub of activity at the heart of the neighbourhood.

Location

Considerations of location are raised at the beginning of this process because it is probably the single most controlling factor in determining *which* form the regeneration of the church *can* take. It will help to avoid the mistake of copying another church's scheme only to find that their location gave them an entirely different catchment and set of possibilities.

Consider the neighbourhood

Is it predominantly residential, commercial, industrial? Is the area one into which people are drawn for shopping, entertainment, homes, work?

The significance of this examination is in discovering what might be the needs of local people that would bring them to facilities in the church building. In an industrial or office area workers may like to visit a café for refreshment or for off-site meetings over lunch. One City of London church with a café does most of its business before 9am when workers drop in to purchase coffee on the way to work and for two hours over lunchtime; it then closes as there is no more real interest from workers for a café – evening refreshments are sought in pubs or restaurants. A successful church café on a busy road in Brixton gave a questionnaire to each customer to find out the patterns of use and so they could then build on them. Parents occasionally dropped in after taking children to school, pensioners came for a healthy lunch, workers had off-site meetings and a sandwich-style lunch.

So the make-up of the church's neighbourhood is important. Residential neighbourhoods will only look for a café if people have reason to walk past the church on a purposeful route. Pensioners may make the church a social destination and look for a healthy lunch. Workers may seek pleasant local convenience with good quality coffee and food.

Plan to undertake an audit. A couple of people with clip-boards can ask two or three questions of passing pedestrians to find out the purpose of their outing and if there is any potential facility in this location that would be attractive to them. Try a weekday and a Saturday. If there are few pedestrians and lots of cars, the church's new activity cannot be based on drop-in interest. Gather information but do not draw any conclusions yet.

Essentially, offering activity with which local people already associate the area, whether leisure, social gathering or work, is a good beginning.

How visible is the church among the buildings that surround it, and is there parking available?

Does the church fit in well, stand out as a landmark, or is it hidden?

The church that is off the beaten track, and especially one that is hidden by trees or other buildings, will need to look in different directions for its new activities than the church that is obvious and easily approachable. People dislike walking through churchyards at night, and don't like dark lanes or industrial areas, but if the activity is attractive enough, the facilities good enough and the parking readily available, then they may come, whether for sport, music or childcare. Pensioners on foot probably won't venture here.

A landmark building in the centre of the town square or the middle of the busy high street can best develop facilities that relate to the many reasons that people are already in the location, much like the 'open door' church on page 22.

Does the community at large know the church and where it is? Plan to test this out by standing in the main street and asking a stranger the way to the church; try old and young people.

What are the communication issues in the neighbourhood?

Who knows what is going on where? Does it have a strong network of community agencies or centres that give it buzz?

List all the community agencies and networks of which you are aware. Often these days the church finds itself outside such networks. Sometimes clergy are represented or informed, but other members of the church have an invisible barrier between their church life and life in their communities. It is time to identify links.

One church made a record of the average hours each church council member spent in volunteering at the church and the hours they spent on other voluntary activity. Not only were they very busy people, but their contacts gave them access to many local charitable organizations that were engaged in working with local people.

Plan later to tap such sources of information on the needs, facilities and activities of local people as seen through the eyes of organizations already engaged in regeneration.

What are the transport links?

Is the church on a bus route, on a main street with lots of adjacent foot traffic?

This question again relates to how people might get involved in activity in the church. If activities are to include the disadvantaged in our society – often not car owners – public transport links are crucial.

Is the church in a conservation area?

If so, there will be an element of pride of place. Is it a 'desirable' area?

Plan to discover such information and the impact it might have on the church's plans. Some activities may be ruled out but others may well then come into play.

Use the collected information to help in the Option Appraisal on page 86.

Report

Report on this element of internal planning by creating a chart. On the left summarize the questions and on the right enter the answers as bullet points. Summarize sufficiently to fit the report on perhaps two pages. Further details that justify the conclusions may be appended.

Summary

Location, location, location! Analyse the location of the church thoroughly. Regenerating the church to work with and for local people requires a clear understanding of every aspect of the location.

Local audit

The local audit will begin with a statistical review of the needs of local people, the current provision in the area. Then find out from local people, community centres and other agencies what community provision is missing and what needs are unmet.

Layers of local audit

Local demographics

There are various sources of local information available. There are government websites, for example, using ward (or Super Output Area) not parish statistics[6] (see www.statistics. gov.uk). These give clear information on the numerical in-

---

6 Use ward statistics rather than parish statistics if the church is likely to make presentations to non-church bodies; outsiders understand council wards and not Anglican parishes. SOAs, or Super Output Areas, are the latest government strategy for identifying areas of deprivation; they are much smaller than wards and give a much more detailed analysis.

formation accumulated from the last census. Other sites give information on indices of poverty and social deprivation that can be extremely useful for identifying large areas of need.

> A vicar arriving in a parish in north London realized from such figures that his parish had a higher ratio of children than almost any other area in the borough; clearly such information leads to questions about provision for children, from after-school clubs to youth clubs and family activities.

Local needs

Demographics identify trends in the local community but do not identify gaps in local facilities and provision. They may help to identify social deprivation but not other elements of social need that are important to building up social cohesion, and ultimately creating opportunity for building up the threads of close-knit and mutually supportive local community. For this other kind of social need there are different sources of information to be tapped. Local community halls and community centres will have information on some of the local demand they cannot meet. If there are more enquiries for children's parties than they can ever meet, then Saturday hall bookings morning and afternoon may be in demand. On one of my church projects researching for a deanery I found that the Area Health Authority had a list of all the voluntary organizations in its area. I selected my area by postcode and wrote to every group asking about the need for facilities and what type of facilities. Most of the answers came from groups trying to meet in inadequate space.

The local CVS (Council for the Voluntary Sector) will have lists of all its members and an even wider mailing list. While the list may not be available to you, an insert to all members or an article in a newsletter may provide useful information.

The local authority's community development department may also have lists and newsletters. Most town halls around the country now provide lists of community halls in their area and information on how to book them. Make contact with each one and find out about their procedures, costs and the size of the space. Ask if the space is busy or whether it is easy to get a booking. Make a chart of these results as the numerical information will be extremely useful later.

Use contacts with local schools and the education department to discover whether there are gaps in provision that the church may help bridge. Many schools may have their own nursery class or even an after-school club, but there can be other gaps that local providers identify.

Social Services, Help the Aged and others may be aware of opportunities with older people. Members of my own church having reached retirement age asked for provision akin to a 'youth club' for older people. Social involvement and physical activity (even walking to the centre) keeps people healthy. With growing numbers of healthy pensioners in our society this is a growing need for provision. An out-of-London church uses its church hall on a daily basis to provide day care for elderly people in order additionally to give respite to carers who are elderly themselves; the provision includes one day with extra helpers when all the clients are sufferers of dementia and other mental illness. This provision, staffed by professional nurses, helps keep people at home with relatives and out of hospital.

The cultural needs of an area are more difficult to identify as no clear source of statistical information exists. Jazz-in-the-Crypt has become a well-known feature of weekend music in south London. Every kind of music finds its way onto the five-days-a-week programme at St James's Piccadilly. Live performance of the arts may be a great addition to local life. But bear in mind that the audience development is difficult to calculate and regular programmes require a great deal of skilled marketing and can very easily make a loss. Several successful churches accept bookings from promoters who pay up-front, £650 per evening for example. In turn these promoters offset their costs with grants from the Arts Council and others. To take this route reduces the church's risk to something negligible. To work with a promoter to bring small music groups, whether jazz or classical, will enable the church to discover whether there is a market for such music. Test carefully, as areas like the West Country may find that there is great demand during the tourist season, maybe even for a partnership with a local pub to supply drinks and food, but that there is little following out of season. Schools and children's music and drama groups may want occasional performance space.

Local provision already in place and planned by others

Find out about local organizers of social and cultural activity. How busy are their programmes? An organization may not have enough participants and be struggling to survive, or it may have more demand than it can handle. Each informs the church steering group about the choices it may need to make. This is very important if church members are convinced that 'because so-and-so does it we can do it too'. There may in fact be far too little demand. Churches putting on classical music events except in the major city centres nearly always struggle to get an audience and hence lose financially. But an occasional or annual church music presentation may pull a big crowd.

Local interviews

Using volunteers, and with information already suggesting a direction, it is possible to do a clipboards-on-the-streets review with local people. Questionnaires that are too open may give a vast list of individual gripes and questions. Use a refined list that reflects the direction towards which the regeneration project is heading. Be specific in your questions because, for example, people with children or noisy families next door always think there is not enough going on for children, even if the local provision is underused; lots of people like the idea of attending music events but would only do so once or twice a year.

For example: 'Do you have children? If St Martha's Church were to open an afternoon club for children would you be interested in using it?' 'What kind of music do you like? If we ran live monthly music events at St Martha's in your kind of music, would you be interested in attending those events? Every time or occasionally?' 'Do you have elderly people in your family who would like to use a day centre but cannot find or get into one?'

Further information

If local trends are becoming more obvious, then double-check with local providers, especially the local authority. For provision for the elderly double-check social services and health-care providers. For provision for children double-check with the youth department, education providers and the children's department of the council and local schools.

Also look again at location. If your church fronts onto a street that is busy with cafés and shops, a community café with charity shop or fair trade shop may fit the church's values and tap into a healthy local market, bringing many people into the church every day.

Are there issues of major significance looming on the horizon that will impact on the lives of local people? For example, major rebuilding of local estates; decisions to be made by estate tenants; new industrial parks being considered; major new housing developments changing the landscape and bringing new people into the area? New roadways or bypasses? How is the church going to consider the change and help local people either to accommodate the potentially good or to oppose the potentially destructive (without becoming negatively NIMBY[7]). Undertake research on all sides of what is happening and remember there is a Christian tradition of backing the underdog or those who are being dispossessed by the process.

---

7 Not in My Back Yard.

Summary

Review the needs of local people and which of those local needs are not currently catered for. Use statistics, local centres and internet information.

Consult

Church members' consultation

Hold a meeting of the church council and interested church members. Give each a copy of the team's report sheets exploring the situation at present.

It is important to the success of the overall regeneration initiative that it is owned by everyone, and achieving ownership is partly based on everyone having access to ideas and decisions. So openness and readiness to record the additional ideas (however wacky) that come from members are essential and this should be done in a way that visibly records everyone's contribution, for example, by noting new ideas and reservations on a flipchart as each page of the report is reviewed. In the Option Appraisal step (below on page 86) only the most workable ideas will survive.

A diagram that I have found most helpful in the development of strategy is 'Forms of Strategy' (see p. 62), taken from *The Rise and Fall of Strategic Planning* by Henry Mintzberg, Free Press, 1994, p. 24. The diagram reflects how it often happens that for effective and creative strategies, new information is absorbed and redundant intentions removed. The overall aim is achieved, but in a different way from the first ideas of how it would work out.

The consultation is just one of the stages of development that may bring new information to the project. We are defining and refining the target as we move forward, consulting with others as we go.

Remember too that consultation is just that, the consultative process is not decision-making; it is a way of collecting the raw material that makes good decision-making possible.

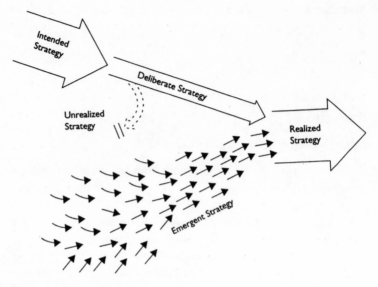

Forms of Strategy

The church is regenerated through re-engagement with its neighbourhood and natural catchment areas, and to achieve this it needs to work in partnership with outside people. The church does not have a valid role as patron of others considered more disadvantaged or less able. We are working in a culture that has mutuality at its core, mutual respect and mutual support. In this context the church that wishes to engage with local people cannot define the terms of meeting or re-engagement but will find the terms of meeting and re-engagement through consultation with local people. So open consultation with real listening means that the listening group, here the team, are ready to allow their own ideas and sense of direction to be altered in order to adapt to the other partners in the regenerated church.

At the meeting, first ensure that everyone has a copy of the reports and everyone has what they need in order to understand it. (Do make large-print copies, and translations, or use preparatory conversations for those for whom a review like this is a strange concept.) Every effort should be made to create a level playing field, with the team providing the materials for coherent review but not controlling the outcomes of the review. Take maybe a third of the time allotted to run through the reports in summary. Take notes if people wish to question the way or why the reports were prepared, not necessarily addressing those issues in the session; get back to those questioners later, their input may be valuable to the process. It is important to be seen to respect the person who has raised the issues and defuse negative challenges with assurance that the team will look at the issue.

Prepare several key questions that look forward, for example:

1 In the light of our church's situation do you see an obvious way forward for our development? All ideas are welcome. New and different ideas are especially welcome.
2 As we look for a new way forward, are there essential values of which we must not lose track?
3 In the light of a new development, what are we afraid we may lose that is important to us individually or as a church?

For the second of these questions you may wish to use the exercise on page 43 about building a new church across the road.

There is a simple principle stated in a book called *The Needs of Children*, by Mia Kellmer-Pringle[8] that says, 'How do I know what I think till I hear what I say?' Many people will not have clearly voiced their ideas for the development of the church – and been listened to – before. Therefore make enough psychological space for them to say what they think and then see its implications or shortcomings and move beyond it. If people offering ideas are attacked or belittled by one or more members of the group, they will become defensive and probably alienated from the development. Bring them

---

8 Mia Kellmer-Pringle, *The Needs of Children*, Hutchinson, 1975.

with you by listening and giving them space to mature their own ideas. The chairperson should actively protect each contribution from any kind of ridicule from others.

State the basic ground rules for a brainstorming exercise, such as:

- Everyone is listened to (go round the circle to ensure everyone has a say even if to endorse someone else's statement).
- No idea can be denigrated by someone else – respect the integrity of everyone's contribution.
- No one may interrupt a speaker, though the chairperson may call time after a while.
- No one can belittle someone else's idea in the group time or even after the session is over.
- Everyone can contribute their reservations with reasons to the steering group during the session or afterwards in a note or conversation.

Brainstorm ideas for the way forward. Look for a wide variety of ideas and value the two extremes of imagination and realism. Imagination will bring new approaches that may not have been tried before. Realism is essential as the way forward is established – but don't let pragmatism short-circuit a good idea that will take time to explore and consolidate.

During Question 1 with ideas listed on the flip-chart (recorded so everyone is seen to have been heard), ask everyone to highlight their preferred ideas (two or three preferred ideas each). Each may add why they like this idea. Still keep the brainstorming rules.

Repeat this process to identify the most important values and subsequently the most dominant reservations or fears. *Note* that many fears are really useful common sense that can be developed later in a Risk Analysis to ensure the protection of the interests of the church during the relatively risky process of change.

After this internal consultation session the steering group should identify the five development ideas with the most support. These will be the centre of interest in the process of developing a solid strategy for the way forward. But keep all the others; it could be that an idea at first marginalized as too dramatic or too expensive will coincide with an outside opportunity that you don't know about yet. For these five ideas make sure that the values of Question 2 and the fears of Question 3 do not rule them out. These five ideas will be used in the Option Appraisal on page 86.

Explore what other churches have done

While it is essential that the steering group visit at least three other churches who have faced and overcome the kinds of challenges you are facing, it can be extremely helpful to open these visits to other church members who can gain vision from seeing the achievements of others. Not all of us are the kinds of intuitive people who can imagine change being good and creative: some have to see to believe.

If possible work in small groups (a carload?) and visit and observe what another church has done to regenerate itself. Information on churches that have undergone either minor or major changes (good and bad) may be available from the secretary to the Diocesan Advisory Committee, archdeacons, bishops and others with roles that involve them visiting various churches.

Ask members of the church visited what they like about the change and what they would do differently if they were to do it again.

Make brief one-page reports to bring back to the church adding the visiting group's likes and dislikes of the development and reasons for their conclusions.

Report

Note each of the ideas. Highlight five or so preferred ideas. Note all key values and fears as well as any key points of discussion.

Summary

Consult church members and keep them engaged in the process.

Collect as many ideas as possible, dismissing none without investigation.

Make sure everyone knows you appreciate their input.

Other stakeholders and their interests

Many churches have friends and well-wishers who are not necessarily committed churchgoers. Make a list of people who are friends of your church and whose opinion and input may be helpful to the regeneration of the church.

Gathering them together may not be as easy as getting church members to gather and talk. Most of these people will have no connection to each other, only with the church, so there are more methods to try.

1 *Personal conversations.* Arrange to meet key individuals, such as the church's patron, and use a one-page summary of the challenge the church is facing in determining to re-generate itself. Ask for ideas and responses to ideas already suggested within the church.
2 *Receptions.* For groups of people, including a few church members, make a simple presentation, maybe around a table, with a similar single information sheet again to en-courage ideas and responses.

In Cycle Two of the development process, this group can be a significant sounding-board, and if they will lend their names to the project it can help the development of funding partner-ships.

Consider consulting others, clergy and lay people, in the deanery or circuit, as they may have valuable experience or recommendations to add to your learning. Find out through local clergy networks, including the ecumenical networks, where people have experience that may be of value, and arrange visits to some of the churches. Then sift all input to identify what is of value to you. Amazing opportunities arrive serendipitously from time to time and entirely unpredictably.

Summary

Write a one-page report on contacts discovered.

Ensure that the friends of the church are able to contribute ideas and suggestions; they may later wish to contribute financially.

Statutory agencies

Developing partnerships with statutory providers can be productive, but the processes on the way are almost always complex if not tortuous. While every such partnership with a local authority is surrounded by legal safeguards and contracts, the development seems most often to depend on relationships with councillors and especially with key officers.

What are the entry points? Published material such as a local authority Unitary Plan[9] may be helpful. Don't be too put off if your church's ideas don't seem an easy fit. Find the relevant names and roles connected to the plan and arrange to see them.

Meeting people has a golden rule: start as high in the organization as you possibly can. If you have contact with (or your archdeacon may provide the introduction to) the Leader of the Council or the Chief Executive, start there. Failing this, I

---

9 A *Unitary Plan* will encapsulate long-term strategy with an umbrella view that progressively carries it into implications for every street and location in the area. It will take into account the local government strategies on the environment, recycling, housing development, street improvement, management of traffic and pedestrians, public transport and so on. Plans for the church's building and site may be implicated in the plan, and before you plan major changes you should know what limitations the Unitary Plan bears for you and what flexibility there might be.

have at times phoned the personal assistant of the Leader or Chief Executive, saying I would like to meet her or him and given a one-sentence explanation. Treat the PA with all the respect you would treat the Chief Executive herself and ask if an appointment may be arranged. Only if I am asked to do I write first. Letters may too easily be side-stepped.

Once arranged, the content of the meeting can be summarized in a description of the development you are undertaking, the review that is its foundation, the research you have done (briefly and in non-churchy language) and the church's wish to work in partnership with others for the good of everyone in the neighbourhood. Of course the church is bringing a major resource to the table – a public building and the goodwill of its members who are local residents – and is now seeking to integrate its efforts with others and work in partnership with others in the area. The response may be a good dialogue about ways and means, ideas of what is already happening and more potential contacts. Ask specifically if there are council targets to engage with or departments to work with.

What has happened commonly as a result of such beginnings is that the council's relationship with the church project is passed to a directorate or officer who will become the council's key contact or development person. Whenever written communication is used to follow up meetings (and make a habit of it), include the Chief Executive or Leader (your initial contact) on the list of copies; this will enable that person to maintain knowledge and interest, and if the church's project comes onto an agenda, for funding, permission or other reason, the key players will be well informed about what is happening. Arrange very occasional update meetings with your first contact and invite them to any special events related to the regeneration project.

The formal development of partnership or funding for projects in church premises will have to be very formal and politically correct. They are complex in order to be robust in the context of the government audit office, that is both fair and seen to be fair. In essence, the church becomes a delivery agent for the council's Outcomes and Objectives, in contractual agreements.

Such processes are often time-consuming but can be very rewarding. It can also happen that you do all the detailed work and attend lots of meetings with the link officer keenly engaged, and the project partnership is turned down at committee stage. Find out from the officer how or whether to present the project again.

Councillors

Councillors have a fairly comprehensive knowledge of their wards and what is happening in the various agencies and centres. They are great supporters but have little power unless they happen to be chairperson of a council committee, where decisions are taken on the many proposals brought forward by officers.

Longstanding councillors may become mayor, which is a role with PR implications, not much power but lots of contacts. They are only in office for a year but may be very helpful during that time.

Council officers

Council officers at more senior levels have power in bringing projects forward to committees who may authorize their progress and the necessary funding. They are definitely people to talk to, but ensure that the officer is at a significantly senior level to make a difference and make recommendations. It was in local authority circles that I first encountered the phrase 'he has risen to the level of his incompetence' to describe people who have risen through the ranks but have reached a level where they do not have the skills necessary to do more than cope. If this is the officer you meet and you begin to realize no progress is being made, be careful how you proceed. No criticism or implied criticism must appear, but try to find another starting-point within the council, using phrases such as 'We don't seem to be finding common ground, we may fit better working with another department.'

Additionally, in every statutory organization there are low-level officers who process paperwork according to detailed agreed practice and whose power is exercised by requiring the letter more than the spirit of the application to be correct. Try extremely hard to deal correctly with every 'i' and 't', but it helps to give time to staff in these roles, that is to recognize their significance and treat them with the respect that seniors more usually gain. Ask their advice, and by their gaining a sense of your respect for them, they may make your path easier.

Directorates

Local authorities often use different names for departments that may be split into a series of directorates, the head officer of each forming a team with the chief executive. These leaders have a great deal of power and run the major departments. Names of directorates vary all over the country but ones commonly of interest to churches can be: Housing, Environment, Community Development (often a sub-section of something bigger) and Social Services.

Community Chest funding

Most local authorities have Community Chest funding. Often funds are released several times annually with a simple application from local groups for small sums of money. This may be helpful to development planning.

The Primary Care Trust/Area Health Authority

With so much preventative healthcare being established around the country it is possible that the area health authority is looking for space for initiatives in communities across their area or is looking for partnerships in making provision for target groups. Make enquiries, again at the highest level you can, with departments that are looking at new developments. The council's social services department may be able to recommend contacts as there is overlap in concern for the disadvantaged in society and projects that are preventative, helping to avoid people needing major interventions.

Education

Both local schools and local education authorities may know of projects or potential partnerships that would like to work with a local church in making provision for children of various ages. Schools may be seeking to establish before and after-school provision but be seeking premises close to children's homes.

Commercial nurseries are often looking for space, but these may be located through estate agents specializing in commercial property. In my diocese the surveyors who do most work for the diocese often know of commercial nurseries seeking premises.

Summary

Councils are the largest spenders on community facilities. They also have major assessments of the needs of particular neighbourhoods and are therefore well-placed partners.

Finding contacts in statutory agencies can be difficult but worthwhile. Ask other churches and voluntary organizations about their successful contacts. Your ward councillor will know a lot of useful people.

Local regeneration initiatives

Since as long ago as the 1980s governments have set aside funds for investment in areas of particular need or poverty.[10] Starting with City Challenge programmes, money was invested in local projects led by local authorities or local quangoes. In

---

10 Teresa Edmans and Grisel Tarifa, *The Regeneration Maze Revisited*, Kings Fund, 2001.

the earlier years the majority of money was spent on capital projects but more recently it has been recognized that projects investing in people required considerable input if the many aspects of social deprivation were to be challenged. For example, people with disabilities have more than just a mobility problem: they may lack work skills, be lone parents, have learning problems or other issues making life difficult. Simply creating a wheelchair-accessible facility is not enough. Multi-faceted community centres that can respond to the variety of needs of clients have always played an important role, for example being accessible, offering advice, providing childcare and providing classes in language, basic education, arts and work skills. The more recent government provision in such funding streams as New Deal for Communities has therefore provided less capital money and far more revenue, and this has been an attempt to pump-prime or fund initiatives that build up the social cohesion of local communities and provide local opportunities for people to tackle their social deprivation.

The streams of funding change regularly. Often they run in three-year cycles. The government websites such as www. governmentfunding.org.uk will give current programmes and guidelines of what is applicable in various areas of the country. There are areas with no programmes.

Partnership potential

The key reason for exploring local regeneration initiatives by central government and local authorities is that, if the church is meeting the objectives of the regeneration board, they can provide partnership funding for projects that benefit the local neighbourhood. At times funding can be 100 per cent of a salary or running costs. Other churches have received funding for small-scale capital projects – replacing the heating system in a church hall and meeting rooms – that will enable new activities to get under way.

Partnership is a key factor here. This is not an organization to which the church can write and get a grant on the basis of an application form. The project will always involve working fairly closely with the regeneration board officers or representatives.

How local regeneration initiatives are organized

The government or local government initiative will be set up as a funding package with a large set of guidelines on the way the money can be used and how the distributing agency should be set up. It will be subject to government audit, and therefore compliance with the complexity of rules must be borne in mind.

Most initiatives are set up at the initiation of local authorities but are managed by a Board that includes a majority of local representatives, with some council officers and people with executive responsibilities. Since such initiatives are for areas of social deprivation, many of the local representatives are inexperienced in the procedures required by government and the process can be frustratingly slow. Most churches usually make good progress eventually. Like some of the Lottery funding schemes, one aspect of the purpose of the funding stream is to empower local people in taking action to improve their own neighbourhoods, and this slow process may be fulfilling one of the aims.

Securing funding for church projects

For the church to participate in partnership with the regeneration programme it needs to become a partner in the process as well as in the delivery of benefits to local people.

To find out about what is going on in your area and how to contact them, try the town hall, local councillor or the Council for the Voluntary Sector.[11] The latter normally know a great deal about local activity and initiatives and at times are responsible for distributing funding. Ask about regeneration initiatives, who to contact and the best way to proceed.

---

11 May be listed under Voluntary Action Council.

Other local churches may include people who have become enmeshed in the regeneration process. Clergy and church members from neighbouring parishes may even be on the regeneration board and be able to advise on how to proceed.

Initial contact will usually be with an officer of the regeneration initiative. Their enthusiasm about your project should be seen in perspective, since the approval for partnership funding for your project will have to come from the regeneration board. Still, the officer can be incredibly helpful in enabling the church to draft a good application form.

Applications for funding are normally long and complex. Bear in mind that central government, local government and regeneration funding is public money and can only be distributed in ways that benefit without discrimination. Therefore if the grant would only benefit Christians it would normally be ineligible, but if it benefits local residents many of whom are Christians (or people of other faiths, of course) then this is fine. Prepare the way by adopting an Equal Opportunities statement and policy. If there are any social groups that the church would not accept in its project then the church may be unsuccessful in its application. I have met a church that was turned down for grants because of their non-acceptance of women priests, though the project was targeting hall refurbishment for local groups.

If this is the first time the church has tackled this kind of partnership then help can probably be found from local community centres, Council for the Voluntary Sector and others; there may even be local workshops run by the council or regeneration body to help groups with the process.

Summary

Discover and contact local regeneration agencies.

Regeneration agencies are into local consultation; going to the consultative forum may bring you contact with the people you should meet.

Look at the regeneration objectives and consider how the church might become a partner in delivering those objectives.

Be politically correct in all your communication.

There are big wins to be had from good partnerships.

Expect mind-numbing amounts of paperwork.

Audit of local groups and organizations

Many churches have run programmes for local residents for generations, from letting space to uniformed organizations to running tea and coffee mornings or parent and toddler groups.

In recent decades, with funding like the Church Urban Fund in place, many churches have set up and run their own community projects, with provision for homeless people, mental health support groups, day centres for the elderly and many more.

A church that seeks to be regenerated may think of setting up a new project for itself, The St Mark's Day Centre for the Elderly, for example, but this is not the only route and may not be the most productive in re-engaging with the variety of local residents. There are ways forward that bring a wide variety of people of all ages and backgrounds into the church.

Consider first that what the church has is surplus building space and times. What existing local organizations and agencies might use this space, bringing their client group with them? The leadership and management of these groups is already in place, and most are set up for paying a letting fee for their use of the space.

Use a list of local organizations and agencies if one is obtainable,[12] to write to each local group in the church's postcode area. You may invite a response to a questionnaire or attendance at a meeting. Lists may not be available and in this case try to get your letter or flier included in a mailing to

---

12 From local authority, health trust or Council for the Voluntary Sector.

the organizations. In one deanery that was reviewing all the church spaces and uses, my letter evoked 40 responses from groups needing space.

Letting space to local groups

If the church might create generic community space such as a hall to let (or may have one main project in mind that would leave additional available time, such as daytime provision for children, leaving the evenings for lettings) it will be worthwhile, as part of the team's overall review of the area, phoning various halls on the council's list to find out the sizes of groups they cater for, the fees they charge and whether they are mostly booked up.

Report on a chart for easy review later:

Centre & address	Numbers accommodated	Cost per hour	Level of bookings

This information will enable the church to set its letting fees at the right level for local people, and comparable with other good provision in the area.

Letting Fees

Generally, if the church sets a letting fee that is comparable to other local community centres this will be acceptable to community groups. It will also be adequate to provide for building maintenance and repair. If a group doesn't want to pay, it is probable that they are not well run and the church may not want them in the space anyway. The logic for saying this is that almost any voluntary groups can get grant aid for setting up, not least from the Lottery Awards for All or the Council's

Community Chest. Running costs may be provided by grants or subscriptions from members.

Some groups coming into the church hall or meeting room may be community businesses like the person who runs exercise classes for a living. These organizers should not expect free space but pay a reasonable amount for the use of space. (Take a quick look at their fees to participants, numbers and times and you will be able to estimate their profits or income per hour.)

Partnerships with other community groups

There may at times be opportunity to develop a partnership that is mutually beneficial. Look out for this possibility as the team contacts and visits local centres and groups.

There are some guidelines to such partnerships that will be worked out in Cycle Two of the Development Cycle.

- Ensure there is a real reason for calling this a partnership: that each partner brings contributions to the partnership that the other does not have.
- The partnership terms should be fair – reasonable and realistic for both groups – and not work to the detriment of either. If the church will be out of pocket without gaining a benefit it is prepared to pay for, this is not a good partnership.
- Ensure that the partner organization is viable and sustainable. Some groups may seek a partnership in order to get discounts on letting fees or other advantages. Review their business plan, annual accounts and bank accounts if they are seeking a lease, as the church will need to ensure they can maintain payments.
- Any partnership that may be long-term should be checked out with legal advisers in Cycles Two and Three of the Development Cycle. Having heard of a possible partnership the team can check out the organization on the local grapevine, with churches and centres, to be sure they are OK.

Information gained in each part of the external audit of possibilities should be well recorded, possibly on a database. I may be a bit of a dinosaur, but I still use my rolodex and index cards for such projects. Record the names of organizations contacted, name of the most helpful contact, phone numbers and other key information.

In a report that will eventually be looked at by the church council and members, make a summary of the positive possibilities that have been raised.

Summary

Identify potential partners, tenants and lettings.

For major partners, check their track record and viability before taking them on.

Other voluntary groups and charities are the outside agencies most likely to understand and be sympathetic to how the church is run and the challenges it faces. They will be good partners.

Building issues to be explored

If the team's Preferred Option has implications for the church building then discussion may begin with the church architect.

If it is a major and possibly innovative intervention in the church building or even its complete replacement, the church may consider inviting several architectural practices to compete (without a fee for the competition) for the work. The secretary to the Diocesan Advisory Committee can advise the team how to go about this later in the development process.

Prepare a statement of need

This is a document useful for presentation to church and other authorities that describes the need for building intervention. In addition to the functions of the regenerated church it should therefore include other essential work such as repairs, the financial and practical reasons for setting out a regeneration plan, the needs and issues of the neighbourhood and the resulting Preferred Option. For Grade I and II* churches this statement of need may be accompanied by a conservation plan to ensure the new works are undertaken with due respect for the heritage qualities of the building and enabling the authorities involved to have the best information available in order to approve or suggest modifications to the plan later submitted to them.

If this is a listed building, it is helpful to meet with the local English Heritage officer and get their opinion on the general direction you are taking. Since English Heritage officers are present at local authority planning meetings as well as church advisory committees, their early input can be extremely helpful.

This is *not* the stage at which to get the architect to work on a detailed design, but it is time to invite the architect to start thinking through with the team the architectural issues the regeneration strategy raises. Build the key points of a brief that outlines needs to be met with regard to function and types of groups and events that will happen in the building. Really you are trying to discover before going further if the team's ideas of uses are physically impossible or are likely to be so expensive as to be silly. For example, one church wanted full disabled access to its crypt, got all the plans drawn up and wanted to raise £450,000 from trusts for the works. This is beyond any kind of sum that outside funders have contributed for this kind of work before and it would be cheaper and more efficient to build something new alongside the church or nearby. This is not an easy option to have chosen!

Begin a dialogue with the *architect* so she or he can incrementally move with the team towards what is needed. Before presenting the Preferred Option to the church council this initial conversation with the architect may provide some reassurance that what the team seeks to do is achievable.

Once the church council has given their approval to the direction of the Preferred Option it will be time to ask the architect to prepare a feasibility study responding to the question: How can we adapt the building for the needs the church is beginning to identify? This includes Health and Safety issues, disability access, toilets, servery and other facilities. Use a list of all the functions of the building during your conversation with the architect, as she/he will then be able to calculate room sizes, extent of the toilet provision, circulation areas and other issues.

The church may wish to add its liturgical reordering to the building works agenda. Ask the architect in preparing plans to keep separate the lists of works for different kinds of function, and ask the quantity surveyor to keep the costs separately identified so the church and any potential outside funders of particular elements of the work can see where money may be spent on different aspects or even phases of work.[13]

In the dialogue with the architect, emphasize minimal intervention for optimum return. Consider reversibility of all changes that are planned, as future generations may have different needs and wish to take out our alterations.

For some meetings that are with outside agencies you may profitably include the architect *not* in determining needs, strategies and potential partnerships, but in *how*, with regard to the building, you respond to those issues.

Also note that it is very helpful to have early meetings (before any detailed design) if you are considering an external extension, especially with planning officers and English Heritage.[14]

---

13 There are very few outside sources for funding for liturgical reordering, while there are lots for providing community facilities. The latter sources usually exclude religious activity, so they want to know that reordering is separately identified and paid for completely separately.

14 For more information of the various authorities to be consulted see Maggie Durran, *Making Church Buildings Work*, Canterbury Press, 2005.

Summary

Prepare a Statement of Need.

Begin a dialogue with an architect but do not ask for any drawing to be done, only ask for drawings when the functions of the new space are detailed.

Explore the ramifications of leases and letting with key people in the diocese.

Legal issues to be explored

Formal applications for permission will not need to be made until the church knows more exactly what it wants to do as the strategy is consolidated. However, there is an advantage to both early consultation with authorities and being prepared well before permission is needed.

An early meeting with the secretary of the Diocesan Advisory Committee should provide some enlightenment. The archdeacon can give further information. When you have outlined the direction the church is taking, she or he will be able to advise you of the routes you may need to take.

Adaptation to the church building will need faculty permission.

Additional uses will need faculty, and to avoid having to apply for faculty for each event a general description of permitted events may advisable.

If the adaptation involves major reordering that will change the balance of use to community or commercial use the recommendation may be that redundancy will be needed, with the residual church space becoming a licensed worship area.

At present leases of consecrated space are not permitted (though lettings are), so creating spaces that will be leased out can probably only be done following the redundancy or partial redundancy route. This particular measure is designed to stop churches alienating part of the building and not being able to get it back from a tenant when they need it themselves in the future.

Planning permission from the local authority may be required if the church's Preferred Option for the building involves change of use. The planning categories allow health provision and nurseries in churches without constituting a change of use, but many other uses will require permission. This will apply to a café, meeting rooms or offices that are not for the church's own use and other activities. Occasional performances are not considered change of use.

Applying for permission from the various authorities is the normal responsibility of the architects, so as we reach building issues in Cycle Two of the Development Cycle, when the regeneration project has a definite form, it will be time not just to enquire but to set up the processes for applying.

Discuss any applications that may need to go to the local authority, as the architect may recommend a preliminary meeting to get advice. If the church is listed, a conservation officer may feel strongly that some changes should not be made. English Heritage, who have a role in all consent procedures for listed buildings, are very aware that churches have to change and develop in order to survive and their local officers may be great supporters when the church is considering physical change to the building.

Other legal issues that may impact on your project include:

- restrictions on use (may date to the donation of the church hall)
- trading
- tax and VAT in particular
- interference with neighbours that will impact on planning permission.

Summary

Ensure the team has a good understanding of all the legal permissions that will be needed and how those will be taken up at appropriate times.

Consider meeting with the appropriate authorities and amenity societies early on in the process to gain their support.

Review

Work on the external elements above may have been undertaken by several people. It is very important to the ongoing coherence and stability of the church's regeneration that that information is openly available within the team and later to the church and other stakeholders.

For every visit or meeting undertaken, create a mini-report with key results as bullet points. Contact names and a note of their responsibilities should be on the report so information can be used again, possibly by another person. (However, outside agencies like to see the same person again, so if you need new skills in the next meeting, take a second person along with the first.)

Among the development team the person with administrative skills will pull these reports into format and if necessary summarize them for general consumption.

With all the reports in front of them the team now ask the question: 'What have we learned?' Some answers may be impressions, but the majority should be factual. 'What information have we gained that limits our possibilities (use the Opportunities and Threats element of the chart on page 85), or that provides openings for us to make progress?' 'Does the information gained enable us to narrow our options down to one leading or Preferred Option?'

The Option Appraisal below enables the team to look at the five or so options that resulted from the brainstorming session and identify what are now the pros and cons of each one. Some may be categorically eliminated. Other decisions may be more subjective. But remember that this recommendations process will next be submitted to the church council, who need more of a rationale than the feelings of team members, so present the rationale before using hunches. For clergy especially it is vital to the longevity of the regeneration of the church that options are not determined by the clergy's power of personality, as the members of the church will need to own and run this project long after clergy have moved to other jobs. If group dynamics such as passive aggression attempt to squash what is an essential development in order for the church to have a future, address the dynamics rather than hurry over them or they will keep resurfacing!

This process should uncover the church's Preferred Option. The remainder of the work on Cycle One is to create a document that shows how and why the Preferred Option fits the requirement of the church and meets the needs and issues raised by local people and agencies.

There are several key elements to the feasibility of the preferred strategy that are elements of this stage of the Development Cycle.

Summary

Use the next steps to identify the Preferred Option to take forward into the next stage of the Development Cycle.

SWOT analysis

A SWOT analysis is a very useful study taken from the world of business. Its strength lies in enabling us to keep a perspective on our internal strengths and weaknesses while at the same time looking at the outside opportunities and threats in our particular context. In the development process we are following, this analysis is placed early in the exploration cycle so that we 'own up' to our internal Strengths and Weaknesses before seeing great Opportunities we want to take but which may play to our weaknesses, not our strengths. It is worthwhile placing it on a sheet on the wall where the group meets so Opportunities can be added later as the exploration cycle continues. You will also discover more limitations and constraints to add to the Threats. This example through the bullet points suggests aspects you should consider in assessing the church's issues.

The team can tackle the exercise first, then ask church members in their first internal consultation to add information on the skills and experience they have to offer. Start by writing in the Strengths and Weaknesses that came up in your analysis of location.

STRENGTHS	WEAKNESSES
• Finance: at least some money available for new initiatives • Building assets • Space • Parking • Play areas • Garden • Existing skills of staff and volunteers • Areas of experience of staff and volunteers such as managing voluntary projects • Business management skills • Financial planning skills	• Lack of money • Lack of skills • Lack of building space • Run-down facilities • Lack of experience • Off the beaten track, not visible • Lack of parking • Lack of local instrument
OPPORTUNITIES	**THREATS**
• 'New Deal' in our area	• New Red Route will disrupt our access • Planning permission will be needed • New road or rail line will disrupt the area

Enter any possible opportunities you already know about, but use this chart during the external search for possibilities, to record relevant information that is collected from the groups and individuals the team members meet.

Report: at this stage prepare a summary diagram fitting on one page, accompanied by the flip-chart page on the wall, to which items can be added later.

Summary

Outlining Strengths and Weaknesses enables the church to play to its real strengths and work to mitigate its weaknesses.

Opportunities and Threats, like location, are qualities of the neighbourhood in which the church seeks greater engagement. Grasp Opportunities and be constructive about Threats.

Option appraisal

Introduction

All projects have some appraisal of options for achieving objectives, that is unless we are extremely short-sighted! There will in the end be a Preferred Option in the forward-looking strategy, but it will have been compared against other options and ideas for measurable values such as the benefits produced and cost-effectiveness. Each option should also be tested against the values of the church to ensure it is the most fitting way to deliver the church's regeneration. *Do not miss this step out!*

> *This outline draws heavily on the overview of appraisal and evaluation available on www.greenbook.treasury.gov.uk*[15]

An option appraisal tells whether a project is worthwhile and it will contain conclusions and recommendations. In summary, once the objectives of the project are established and summarized, the possible options for the way to achieve those objectives are identified and listed and the cost and benefit of each is then analysed. The ideas or options come from the team's work, the church brainstorming, and suggestions of the stakeholders, and will be added to the recommendations of outside agencies and residents.

---

15 This chapter will not explore all the elements in the Greenbook, but the full text is fascinating in its detail. For churches considering an application to the Heritage Lottery Fund it is advisable to read it all.

Cycle One: Exploring the Possibilities

The initial setting up of the framework for option appraisal is here in Cycle One because it will inform the research into outside agencies and organizations. Possibilities will be far less random and more readily sorted by the team in the context of a framework for appraisal.

Justifying action

There are two fundamental prerequisites for change, and these are that the needs will be met and that the proposed intervention is likely to be worth the cost. In our case the internal need for change, that is to the church and its members, may be seen either in a new drive for mission and ministry or in the slow decline of the church, and this can be itemized or quantified. To outside agencies and partners and eventual funding partners, the predominant need will be in the local community and again that can be itemized and quantified. Against this the project has to be worth the cost, that is that the benefits it will produce to meet the needs are at an appropriate, realistic and acceptable level of cost.

Research is the first step.

Consider each bullet point for the internal needs of the church and then for the external needs of local people.

- What is the cause of the failure that led to the need for change? (In the church it may be falling numbers, decaying building or poor levels of fundraising, or many other factors. Outside it may be high levels of unemployment or job opportunities or lack of social cohesion and social gathering places.)
- Current and projected trends. If the present trends were to continue what would be the picture over the next few years? An internal assessment may be made from the church's own records. The external assessment may be made from the work of local authorities and others such as the Area Health Authority. (These larger agencies for change have planners whose job it is to project such trends, so if you are setting out on what may be a large project in the church,

the research you undertake in visiting outside agencies will enable you to gather this information.)

• Disadvantaged groups and individuals (statistics) and potential beneficiaries.
• What would be the result if nothing changed or if there were to be minimal change?

Setting objectives

Set out the desired outcomes and objectives in order later to identify all the options for meeting them. First, outcomes are the benefits to society that may come from the proposed church regeneration. There should be a way to measure the outcomes over time to prove that the church has delivered what it intended to. If you are planning to ask outside funders to help the church, defining outcomes is the best starting-point.

Perhaps examples are the easiest way to illustrate outcomes:

Outcomes

1 Improved community relations:
   • Reduced damaging activity by young people, vandalism and anti-social behaviour
   • Greater participation in community and civic life, with the church providing opportunity for community functions and meeting space
   • Promoting good relations between local people
2 Improved employability:
   • Improved basic skills, for young unemployed to gain work-related skills; for women seeking skills to enter the job market; literacy and numeracy
   • Improved educational opportunity; working closely with local education providers we will enable people to gain the skills and confidence to go to college
3 Improved personal independence:
   • Developing skills for local homeowners (many are first-time owners) in DIY and in employing builders for repairs and improvements

- Out-of-school programmes for children, improving educational attainment
4 Increased voluntary and community capacity:
  - Better services will be on offer. Staff will have the skills to support and develop voluntary groups and local initiatives; support in the development of management of community programmes
  - Improved capacity of services with educational, cultural, heritage and health events and programmes for people of all ages
  - Increased provision of meeting space, especially a large event space for meetings and social gatherings
5 Reduced isolation:
  - Women who have been at home with young children will gain social and educational opportunity through support in education and training, through the community resource centre, through the variety of social and cultural opportunities
  - People of all ages will have greater social and cultural opportunities
  - Young people will be supported in making their way into the workforce through targeted educational and training programmes
  - Social, health and well-being programmes for the elderly, with some targeting ethnic minority elderly who are under-represented in local provision
6 Increased and supported cultural identity:
  - The large meeting space will provide opportunity for a variety of cultural activities that will support cultural identity and social and cultural cohesion
  - Heritage programmes will affirm the stories and histories of local people and through a programme of exhibitions and events build up a greater sense of community between people from a variety of backgrounds.

This is a rather long list of outcomes prepared by a church in the north of England that was working with partners to create a new community centre inside its walls. Many of the outcomes can be measured: from lowering crime figures to people transferring to the local college or getting jobs. Lettings for community events can be counted along with the numbers attending.

You may not yet be able to list many of the outcomes of benefit to local people, as you have yet to research what is needed specifically, but once you start researching the needs of local people (see page 136) you can begin to describe your project in terms of its targeted outcomes.

Outputs are steps on the way to achieving the outcomes, and these outputs can be measured. One obvious output could be a repaired and adapted building, or the establishment of an activity programme. Each is a means to an outcome.

Setting *targets* can be a helpful process in achieving first outputs, then outcomes and finally overall objectives. Targets should be Specific, Measurable, Achievable, Relevant and Time-bound. The acronym SMART is commonly used.

For example:

Purpose: for St Ethel's Church to re-engage with its neighbours to our mutual benefit

Outcome: improved quality of community services for local people, contributing to social cohesion and community spirit

Output: to adapt St Ethel's church building with facilities that make it suitable for use for community meetings and events

Target: to raise £200,000 by next year for building work

Appraising options

Create a wide range of options for consideration. The team's activity in meeting with the church members and with other stakeholders will have generated many ideas. The external part of Cycle One of the Development Cycle: Exploring the Possibilities will result in yet more ideas to add to this process.

It is advisable to set up a framework into which each idea is fitted and by which comparisons can be made.

Then as many as possible of the ideas generated are assessed as options, to make sure that no good idea is left out too early in the process. Keep 'do the minimum' in the option list, even as the list gets shortened, so you can keep a positive perspective on each item on the list compared with where you are.

The team will soon need to move off this chart and make a summary page of each option using the headings from the chart. They may of course add their own headings.

Costs

As the development process moves on through Cycles One to Three, more work will be done to refine estimated costs. It is preferable to compare costs at the present value unless there is a very significant reason for not doing so. That means the team will find out the cost of building adaptations or for another option the cost of a new building at today's prices. Similarly a community programme of projects can be costed today and a note can be added that future years can expect inflation to make an impact on the budget.

Many benefits do not have a numeric value that will enable direct comparison, but notes should be added. Some such values will have greater weight for church members than others. For example, some kinds or activity may fit more comfortably into a church for aesthetic or cultural reasons. Certain types of music may feel fitting to a church building, and this cultural value of say classical music over jazz or world music should be stated. Discussing the values associated with particular benefits will enable you to dismiss any spurious ones. There may be elitist or racist attitudes that you will want to address early on! Some people may, because of unspoken cultural values, automatically eliminate certain options without thinking; the chart system will help avoid this.

Option	Benefits to the church	Benefits (measurable)	Benefits (not measurable)	Disadvantages to church
1. Do minimum	No increased effort	None	None	We are drifting towards closure

Adjustments to the Option Chart

Distribution considerations

Some benefits may have greater impact for certain people because of their socio-economic group, their ethnicity, their age or their gender. Consider whether some types of people will get more benefit than others.

Price changes

Changing technology, price rises, wage rises, recession or a boom economy may have an impact. For churches planning building works it is important to work from a properly calculated budget from a quantity surveyor which the surveyor may adjust for annual building cost inflation.

For community programmes take the base figures from an actual community project in the area (their annual report will almost always be available with such figures). Do not guess.

Disadvantages to local people and environment	Capital cost	Ongoing revenue cost	Fitting with the church's values	Reason for dropping this option
Loss of opportunity	None	Maintenance and repair will increase while income does not	Not fitting with the gospel call to mission	Not sustainable for the future of the church

Required rate of return

Some agencies and funders will compare the relative value of projects requiring funding by looking at the rate at which a benefit is provided. This is critical when approaching outside funders; churches often ignore it and may still succeed through internal fundraising, where relative cost may be an issue.

For example, a church will provide community facilities in its building for 100 people each day at a capital cost of £400,000. The local authority can build a new community hall in the next street for £600,000 serving 200 per day. The latter is clearly a better rate of return, costing 75 per cent of the church cost *per person*. This can be altered by other issues: the church facilities (well maintained) may be designed for a 30-year life span and the hall for only 20 . . . and so on. But comparisons will be made, so the church that plans to fundraise outside its own circles will want to consider options with a realistic rate of return.

Risks

A format for risk analysis is set out below on page 106 and as the list of options is reduced so the risk analysis may help inform the team of the optimum way forward. For example, some options may have low capital cost, and there is a relatively lower risk of the church being unable to raise the money to make it happen.

In sophisticated major projects risk can be reduced to numerical values and for a large capital project the quantity surveyor and project manager can undertake a risk analysis.

For example, if the regeneration project may involve new construction there is a risk of archaeology becoming an issue. If the risk is medium – we know there are burials in the area – then the risk may be reduced by digging a trial pit to assess the archaeology before starting construction.

Bias

Note that your team may be full of optimists. Their tendency will be to play down the risk, suggest unrealistically low costs and undervalue the disadvantages. Also they will tend to manoeuvre their favourite option onto the list even after its disadvantages have proved to be great. Be open and discuss bias fully, as it always clouds judgement.

Sensitivity

More complex projects, and those being presented to a major funder such as the Heritage Lottery Fund, will require an analysis of the sensitivity of the figures the team have devised.

Simply, there are always unavoidable future uncertainties that will impact on the project and on the options the church chooses for the way forward. Some non-financial impacts could be: the vicar leaving for a new job in the middle of the development, and this *always* has a major impact, normally derailing the project; a new road or estate being built nearby;

a change in diocesan policy requiring a change in personnel or finance at the local level.

From a financial point of view a change of government in local or national elections could change the priorities of a local regeneration agency such that funding becomes unavailable; or the change of government policy could decimate the voluntary sector as it did in the later 1980s and early 1990s making funding for community projects more rare than hen's teeth, with projects closing all over the country.

When creating the revenue figures for a community hall or facilities, project various levels of take-up for space to be let and consider the impact of a lower level of lettings on the viability of the project. A bit of bad publicity could be unavoidable and make such a drop happen. So it is advisable to set rates that result in lettings for say 60 per cent of the time being sufficient to cover all costs, that is a lower break-even point.

The option with which the church proceeds will be decided in the light of a judicious view of the sensitivities of each option and the potential of impacts that cannot be controlled.

Affordability

Can the church afford the option? For the capital phase of each option that involves building works an assessment can be made of the sum of money the church has already plus a *very realistic* sum from outside fundraising. In the present funding climate, the money available from trusts and foundations can be ascertained from trust guides online or in books. Add to this the current maximum available from Lottery funds and the sum becomes clearer. To create further perspective the cost per square metre of building works has to be seen to be sensible and affordable in comparison with parallel projects, in charity as well as church sectors.

For a capital project expect to have an *indicative budget* for each shortlisted option.

One church had begun preparation for setting up business start-up premises alongside the continuing church. As soon as the first budgets were generated, it was clear that the cost of adapting the building to meet regeneration agency target provision was double the amount of capital the regeneration agency was prepared to make available for capital works. It was unaffordable.

For the revenue part of a project (and ongoing revenue projections are required for most capital investments to prove that regeneration provision is sustainable) a *cashflow* should be prepared when looking at a shortlist of options. This will show the full cost[16] of running the building or the project and show from where the income to meet those costs is coming. Some church projects are self-financing through lettings (include letting rates and hours of use to justify this income), others such as arts projects are grant-dependent and some justification for optimism about grant income should be available.

Funding statement

This should show which church sources, partners and other organizations will provide resources. As you go through the development process differentiate between money in the bank, money promised and money hoped for.

Summary

Only when more information is gathered and more external auditing is undertaken will the team be able to decide what is possible and realistic as well as desirable.

Do not decide between these options at the outset but at intervals during this process as more information is gathered to remove unworkable options from the list.

---

16 More explanation of how to prepare cashflow projections is available in Maggie Durran, *The UK Church Fundraising Handbook*, Canterbury Press, 2003.

Identify all options and systematically appraise them against:

- The values of the church
- The benefits produced versus cost effectiveness
- Justification
- Costs
- Distribution of beneficiaries
- Risks
- Rate of return (can it be done better or more effectively?)
- Sensitivity to future changes
- Affordability.

Review the church's resources

In the preparation elements above, the team was encouraged to consider the church's existing resources of people, buildings and money that might be dedicated to the regeneration of the church. With the Preferred Option coming to the fore it is now possible to begin to match up resources and needs in regeneration activity and identify where new resources will be needed.

Review the resources, such as space, staff time and finances, that the church has available and how well they are used and might be used. Consider new provision you can or might be able to make, in the light of current resources. (See *Making Church Buildings Work* for more explanation and exploration.[17])

Assess management needs for potential developments. What can be managed in-house (consider volunteers and staff): for the building, for the centre, for projects, for leases and letting? What professional skills will be needed or are already present? Create a team to work with the vicar rather than assuming the vicar should direct or control everything. Don't make the mistake of thinking that as the vicar is the president at the liturgy that they make the best manager or the only leader.

---

17 *Making Church Buildings Work* (see n. 14).

First consider the ongoing management committee and the skills and experience which will be helpful to its good functioning. When the management is set up in detail in Cycle Two of the development planning tool, more details will be prepared, but some outline thoughts now will help the development team respond constructively to questions and ideas from the church council.

Briefly outline the skills and resources of these different areas and the professional qualities needed, so the church council can take an informed direction. Some activity that has previously been done by volunteers may now become part-time or full-time jobs. The church administrator may already be busy and any increase in booking procedures and lettings may require a hall administrator, perhaps part-time. Often clergy function as keyholders, letting in visiting groups and locking up when they leave. With a busy building this will certainly have to pass to someone else, such as a caretaker, in a new job that may be full-time.

While there is time in hand during the development of the regeneration project, it could be helpful to review management experience and skills with a view to finding training in areas where this is lacking. Being a good employer or a good line-manager requires both basic knowledge and skills and usually experience as well. Many clergy have more academic backgrounds and have not had to undertake systematic annual appraisals with staff. Also they work such irregular hours themselves that they may not readily realize the importance of time-keeping and job descriptions among their more 9-to-5 staff. Training will help. There are two main approaches. First, organizations like the Directory of Social Change specialize in all kinds of training for charities, including management of organizations and staff. Members of the projected management committee can sign on to these courses. Second, and more expensive, the trainers who run events for training organizations can be booked to run dedicated day workshops for charities. In this way all the committee can be trained in the variety of responsibilities they will take on.

Consider additionally that the kind of accounting currently undertaken for the church may not be adequate for the regeneration projects being set up. With church accounts, a simple annual budget and occasional reports on progress through the year may be adequate. But with a busy programme every day, with different budget headings, there may be a much more complicated picture. If there are staff to be paid and letting or trading income is to provide the money for their salaries and utilities and overheads, then the committee may need both a more comprehensive budgeting system and simple management accounts to keep a careful eye on progress through the year. *A Practical Guide to Financial Management* by Kate Sayer-Vincent[18] is a useful tool for those who have no experience or to provide models for treasurers taking this on. If the church is going to be busy every day, like the marketplace church on page 25, it may possibly require the services of a part-time book-keeper for say half a day each week. Most urban centres have small accounting companies for individuals who work freelance for a variety of clients on this kind of basis; this may be sufficient to keep all the financial reporting up to date for the committee and highlight any emerging problems, especially with cashflow, in the early stages of new programmes.

Projected revenue

Again, a useful exercise before presenting the Preferred Option to the church council is to make a first projection of the revenue figures of the regenerated and busy church.

Take the information gained by contacting local halls and community centres. Extract the rates for letting a space or spaces of the size or sizes the church may be letting and any the team are proposing to lease out, and start with a proposed letting rate or rates. Merging these rates with your proposed

---

18 Kate Sayer-Vincent, *A Practical Guide to Financial Management*, Directory of Social Change, 1998.

schedule of use (the hours the spaces will be booked), you can calculate the income that will be generated when the church or church hall is busy.

Using the present church and hall running costs as a starting-point, project the costs of the busy regenerated church. Salaries for new staff may be calculated using the job ads in the local paper. Remember to add National Insurance and other salary costs, including recruitment. Utilities may be calculated by multiplying present costs: a church heated seven days may be five times the present cost, and so on. Your insurance cost may increase; seek advice. The new space will be advertised and promoted locally. Administrative costs will rise.

Combine both projected revenue income and projected costs into a cashflow projection, monthly at first, with subsequent years showing quarterly. Always work with the next twelve months from today broken down by months. At the bottom of the budget note the opening and closing balances. The opening balance is the sum in hand (or at the bank) from the previous month. Add this month's projected income and subtract this month's expenditure to give a month-end figure.

You can now tell if the projected income from letting and leasing (or other sources of income) is going to be adequate. As you progress through the months (an Excel or Lotus 123 spreadsheet will give you immediate information), there must never be a negative figure in the cashflow projection, as you must always be able to pay staff and other costs you have incurred. Much fuller information on preparing a budget and cashflow projection is shown on pages 151ff.

If your projection is showing negative figures anywhere on the cashflow, then two considerations are possible. One consideration is that the overall income may be inadequate, and it may be necessary to increase the letting rate to cover costs. For many churches and church halls with groups that already are concerned at costs, it has proven possible to raise the letting fee for evenings and even more for weekends when there is greater demand by bigger groups. It is even possible to have a lower rate maintained for children's groups such as uniformed organizations, but to keep the higher weekend rate for weekend children's parties. The second consideration is that during the setting-up period the new everyday regenerated church may have fewer bookings and lettings than needed to cover the costs during that period. There are more possible solutions. The church (or diocese) could loan a start-up sum to the regeneration project to get things going; a careful examination of the allocated costs may indicate that apart from promotion, many costs will only grow at the rate of new use and these can be carefully adjusted on the budget. Note too that a church cannot justify running community facilities at a loss, and no outside funder is going to be interested in providing capital to loss-making community facilities, so spend some time resolving these issues.

The cashflow projection is more accurate than a simple budget as it responds to the variations in months over a year. For example, you will pay utilities quarterly, and that means some months have higher payments than others, so income in preceding months must be higher to cover that larger expenditure. And if the insurance payment of several thousand pounds becomes due early in the year, the cashflow must be adequate to cover it.

In terms of ongoing financial structures:

1 Letting and leasing church community facilities. This is considered investment of resources by the Charity Commissioners. Therefore it is unnecessary to have an entirely separate structure. But this activity is very different from the normal religious activity of the church. So it is advisable to have a properly constituted sub-committee of the church council (covered by written terms of reference) with its own sub-committee budget and pages in the annual accounts. This allows the sub-committee to focus and bring together the particular skills and experience they require and also prevents the new community facilities becoming a hidden

drain on church resources that are restricted to its religious activity.

2 Other activities may be trading. Any activity from café to charity shop that it is not appropriate for a charity to undertake. Not only are they not within the objects of the charity, but they engage in activity that is vulnerable to market changes that could put the charity's main budget at risk. Therefore the finances of trading activity should be set up as a limited company that ultimately would not affect the church/charity if it became insolvent.

These structures may be explored early in the development process, now that the outline of the Preferred Option has been determined. By the end of Cycle Two of the Development Process, many more details can be made firm, whether for letting rates, community projects to be run in partnership or the income from property leased for the longer term.

Summary

Review the resources you will need and the resources you have available to meet those needs.

Assess skills and tasks to be done and identify gaps.

Consider a budget for running a changed building, including increased staff, as this will inform the team about how much of the new building is let to make income for ministry and how much is used for ministry.

Report to the church council

The first major report to the church council at the end of Cycle One is a critical stage in the project's progress. In Cycle Two, expense will begin to be incurred, so the church council will need to ratify the direction proposed and support this with the funding that is needed for further progress.

The report should be simple and straightforward enough for comprehension by every member of the church council (even if some may need a little extra help with the implications) but have enough appended backup information that the most inquisitive may find the grounds for the report's conclusion on the Preferred Option. Do not depend on winning people over by a verbal presentation. If the Preferred Option cannot be stated clearly enough, review whether it really is the best or only option, that is revisit the selection stages if necessary.

1 In an executive summary state the Preferred Option and the reasons it is preferred:
   • Original input including the values of the church and mission action points
   • Needs of local people
   • The demands of local people (that is where they want to make change in their lives and how they want to change)
   • Synchronicity with mission plan
   • Synchronicity with potential partners.

2 Expand the key points to cover the outcomes of the regeneration project using the Preferred Option:
   • Outline the main ongoing activities that will be undertaken.
   • Outline the outputs that will be achieved (outputs are explained more fully on page 121).
   • Outline your projected inputs that will be required to make the Preferred Option work, such as staff, finance, building alterations, changes to the church's existing activities and programmes.

3 Outline the activity that will be involved in Cycle Two of the development so that the tasks of the project team, confirming all elements of the Preferred Option, are understood.

4 List key decisions with the reasons that they will need
to be made by the church council in the near future, for
example:
  - Consideration of the sale of property from which
    money is essential to the regeneration of the church.
    Explain how its asset value may be maintained (or lost)
    in the process.
  - Consideration of any liturgical reordering that may be
    a by-product of the regeneration, noting that we are
    not at the design stage, but that early warnings make
    for smoother processes later.

Explain the relationship qualities of working with many
of the potential partners the team may have identified;
therefore nothing is in the bag, it is all edging forward.

Identify and illustrate the link between the Preferred
Option and the viability and sustainability of the church
in the long run. Summaries of the early draft of projected
cashflows may be used to indicate how the team plans to
achieve this.

The variety of individual summary pages produced by team
members during the exploration cycle should be available
to church council members, though not everyone will want
them. Either attach copies to everyone's prepared material or
make a few copies available for those who want to take them
away to read them.

One significant decision is required by the team from the
church council as a result of this meeting, and that is general
agreement on the way forward and commissioning the team
to continue into Cycle Two, which will build up partnerships
and mutual commitments that should not be readily broken
and will begin to incur costs, such as architect's fees for feasibility work.

It is recommended that the church council has at least half
a day for this meeting, as it is important for the regeneration
project to be owned by everyone, even though it is being

engineered by the team. A half day will allow everyone to make observations, offer ideas, present fears and point out limitations. Make sure that one of the team is taking good notes, and record as much as possible on flip-chart sheets.

End the session with a Risk Analysis on the Preferred Option (it can be refined later) with everyone making a contribution to the implications of the direction, and mitigating action that will increase the stability of the way forward.

Risk analysis

Filling in a summary of risk analysis is a great tool for looking at the downside of a good idea. The team that has come up with a recommendation for the way forward is bound to be enthusiastic about it, and at every opportunity will want to promote and even defend the idea. However, ensuring that the way forward is made as 'risk-free' as possible should be systematically addressed. In working with church congregations, I find that this exercise more than any other puts the fears of church members into perspective; most can be seen to be sensible and practical reservations rather than emotional reactions.

All risks are entered in the left-hand column, I have entered a few possible examples. *The likelihood of risk* is how likely we think it is that this problem will arrive: medium, low or high. The *impact* question is crucial, as this describes how much effect this risk would have on the future of the project. High impact suggests it could kill off the project. A practical example of this could be having the right insurance for a new activity; while the likelihood of not having insurance may be low, the impact of not having insurance in the case of a problem could be devastating not just to the project but to church life as well. In the fourth column there is a list of actions that will *mitigate against this risk* becoming a major problem. Here sensible planning and safeguards are listed.

The Risks we list at this Cycle of the Development Cycle relate particularly to the whole process of developing a strategy and ensuring that all aspects are well covered. By Cycle Three of the Development Cycle, the Risk Analysis should cover the ongoing running of the regeneration project.

The risk	Likeli-hood of risk	Impact of risk	Mitigating action
That the church won't be able to afford the new strategy	High	High	1 New work won't be started till money is in place from fundraising. 2 Financial planning will be undertaken and checked for viability and sustainability. 3 The architect will be briefed to create new facilities while keeping costs down. 4 All decisions with financial implications will be thoroughly discussed by the church council.
That our partners won't be as good as they seem at first	Medium	High	1 We will check out significant partners and potential leaseholders thoroughly, taking up references, reviewing their accounts and their business plans. 2 We have looked at lots of possibilities before making up our minds and will continue to consider new options that arise.

The risk	Likeli-hood of risk	Impact of risk	Mitigating action
That our church building will be spoiled	Medium	Low	1 All plans from the architect will be subject to church council approval and approval of outside authorities including the Diocesan Advisory Committee and faculty.

Consultation and listening

I have just come from a meeting where church members were angry and frustrated over a new hall development. I was invited to help by chairing it, and this reinforced for me the importance of understanding consultation and listening.

It is useful to have meetings more often if church members are collectively unsure about the development. There are some clear aids if such meetings are to move towards a creative co-operation between the team and the other members.

1 It is well worth carefully choosing a chairperson who can be dispassionate about the project and the issues involved, maybe even someone from outside the team and the church. It should not be anyone who will become defensive about the process or possible solutions. Their most effective tool is to communicate that the team is listening, everyone wants to hear from all those present and the team is noting down everyone's questions, ideas and criticisms to ensure that nothing creative is lost.

2 The church members must have accepted early on that change has to happen, or they will find fault with every

solution, seeing it as an enemy to their peaceful continuation in the present. Persistent resistance may require that the church's need for regeneration is presented again, with a request that people consider solutions and these solutions can then be shown to work or not work, rationally and systematically. Listen hard, as an easier solution than the one the team is chasing may come forward. Above all, the chair's job is to ensure that the team listens and everyone gets to speak. The team may offer points of information or indicate that they have researched this issue and give their results. They may offer copies of their summary reports and detailed information-gathering where this would be helpful. But avoid arguing with dissenters as this will make a difficult situation worse.

3 When criticisms are the first items raised by those present, move along to asking for further ideas and particularly to engage them in enabling newcomers, who will be in church because of the project, to be inspired and introduced to the Christian faith by what is around them.

Pastoral care

There may be church members who are fragile or vulnerable people for whom change is intensely distressing. The team should be able to pass these people over to the care of the church's pastoral team. If the vicar is champion of the project and a chair of presentations, it is very difficult though not impossible for the same person to listen to and support such individuals who are having trouble with change. Reassurance is fundamentally about unchanging relationships and an unchanging God in the middle of the confusion this person feels. If the church building and its patterns may change significantly then house groups for fellowship as well as prayer and Bible study may be able to offer structured support for individuals.

Individual conversations

There will always be some church members whose areas of skill and experience result in more questions than there are answers.

Building professionals in the congregation may bring the most challenges.

- They understand what may go wrong! They may fear that the nightmare cases they have experienced in their career can happen again in the church. It is worth having an individual conversation, or later holding a meeting with the architect and design team, for these professionals to realize that a project is being well managed and will be delivered effectively and efficiently. And if their questions help clarify what might have become a problem, or highlight an issue no one had yet foreseen, this will be to everyone's benefit.
- Professionals may be used to managing building projects *and* not being the client; they may be very poor clients – they may interfere too much or criticize unnecessarily. Only have a building professional on the team if they are able to operate 'hands off'.
- Not all professionals are great at their job. I have stories of churches who have let an architect from the congregation manage a project, and then it has run months over time and thousands over budget and they are impotent with regard to the outcome. It is far better to listen to the professional's advice and then ask the same questions of the design team later to ensure the issues are covered.
- Whether great at their job or not, not all architects or surveyors are experienced at working on heritage buildings such as churches, so even if their knowledge of process and contracts may be helpful, they may not be the best designers of new interventions in the building.

Other professionals in the congregation may have parallel concerns. The business manager or accountant may be more interested than most to run through the details of the regeneration project business plan. Again their value may be best used as an informed observer. Not every business person has the right balance of entrepreneurial skills for every type of business, nor are they always up to date on business practice. Keep an open mind and listen hard, question and learn.

Summary

The church members and church council should be fully apprised of how and why the Preferred Option has been chosen. This should produce a consensus on going forward.

- Prepare a simple summary report stating the Preferred Option and reasons for its adoption; the next steps; append as much detail as possible.
- Record all discussion, especially about the steps.
- Make a risk analysis.
- Consult and listen!
- Be prepared to show a reminder of the case for change. (Don't start with this, or you risk spending the whole meeting on it!)

8

Cycle Two:
Design and Plan

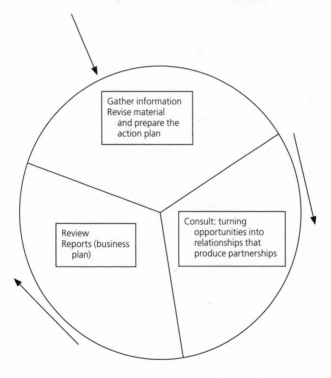

With a great deal of groundwork complete both inside the church and in the neighbourhood, the way forward is becoming more certain. The Preferred Option of Cycle One will in Cycle Two become the actual Strategy, or if the detailed planning shows it to be ultimately unworkable, a further option can take its place.

The consolidation that is the theme of Cycle Two involves revisiting various elements to take them forward to agreement with the many players involved. Both internally with regard to structures, job descriptions, tasks and legal accountabilities the plan needs to be teased into the form which in Cycle Three will become the working document steering the construction and implementation of the church's regeneration.

Team development: preparing the action plan for the second cycle of the development

The church team can now plan its work in the next cycle of development. Potential partnerships will be developed further and from the church's point of view these may also form long-lasting friendships. The person who made the initial contact with a potential partner may now take more members of the team to any meetings in order to widen the team's ability to respond to the detailed issues that will be raised; the answer to many questions may be 'I'll make a note and find out about that' or 'I can ask the church members (or council) to consider that.' The initial relationship may have been brokered by the team's champion but now it's time to bring along those who work systematically and in detail. Each person has their strengths and I for one am always relieved to leave meetings about legal details to other people!

The steering group/team now has the support of the church council to proceed to the more serious development around the Preferred Option which I am now going to refer to as the Strategy; in Cycle Three it will become the Plan. Recollecting the diagram on page 62 the team will now consolidate its strategy, ensuring that ideas raised in Cycle One research are dropped when they can be seen to be impossible, and that ideas coming in that will alter the church's own strategy are really appropriate to the church's regeneration and that every aspect of the strategy is appropriately explored and dealt with. This will involve, for example, redoing the SWOT analysis focusing closely on the confirmed Strategy and a more comprehensive risk analysis. Some such studies will be continued after the external element of Cycle Two has further clarified elements of the strategy.

The reports of Cycle One have till now focused on the church council, and religious language and concepts have been important. With external partners now entering the Strategy in a serious way, the Strategy will be embodied in a business plan that uses the language and concepts of the statutory and voluntary sectors. When negotiating with local authorities and regeneration boards, a further language and set of concepts comes into play – a kind of government-speak – that will be embodied in guidelines and application forms for grant aid. Look among the church membership for anyone who works in local government or local authority departments, as they may be able to help in turning the church's reports and material into the language of the sector.

The Strategy will also be developed with assurances and testing of its viability in practical ways. The finances set out above (page 91) will now have a more rigorous review for presentation. The management plans will proceed so that by Cycle Three required jobs may be advertised, policies set in place and written up, and tenancy agreements signed.

Summary

Look over all the elements of Cycle Two and work out how the team is going to break the work down into tasks and allocate these tasks to individuals. Set timescales for achieving the tasks and a programme indicating when the team expects the tasks to be completed.

Gather information

Location

Review the location issues (see page 53) and ensure that nothing is being missed just because newer information has been secured. There may be good reasons given by some of those consulted for thinking that people will come to the church although it is off the beaten track, but now is the time to double-check. If, for example, a health centre will relocate into the church premises then a lot of people will come out of necessity, it can be depended upon. But a hairdresser or social group that depends on people coming voluntarily and not of necessity will still be a problem. On the other hand there are activities where expert and effective marketing can make the difference; as part of the developing Strategy check the skills and track record of fledgling projects or businesses that are seeking space. One church that was totally hidden by high-rise council blocks had a very effective pensioner project move into its hall and succeed because of the skills and connections of the project, and its ability to transport people by minibus to the hall. In this case the local authority was paying the rent to the church and funding the workers.

The location of a retail initiative such as a church café is often set up on the basis of hopelessly optimistic plans, especially for numbers of customers. For such a trading initiative, a business plan is an essential tool for testing out and proving the viability of the project.

Summary

Review all the key issues on location; this is a make-or-break item.

Church council input

Review the material and notes collected from the consultation with the church council at the last meeting. Ensure that these are incorporated into the body of the Strategy and useful material is appended.

Note any reservations that were expressed in the church council meeting and keep in mind the possibility that these may become key issues later when you work on the critical path: could they actually be problems that stop the progress of the project?

Building issues: continuing dialogue with the architect

Once the church members and church council have approved the direction of the team, conversation with an architect may begin.

If the Strategy involves major or dramatic change to the church building then it may be worth inviting several architects, including the church's own Inspecting Architect, to offer ideas on how they might tackle the design challenge. It is possible to use an architect other than the inspecting architect for any discrete piece of work.

This process is covered in greater detail in *Making Church Buildings Work*.[19]

An architect responds to the client's brief. In this first conversation with the architect bring her or him up to speed on the Statement of Significance (see page 50). This will ensure that respect for the quality of the building and the context in which change is being made takes on a proper perspective. Along with this the architect should be given an initial brief that describes new facilities in the following terms:

- Kinds of new and existing use (liturgical use, type of events, types of groups)
- Times at which each kind of use is in the building
- Numbers in each group on average and the occasional maximum (such as weekly congregation and the increased number for festivals)
- Particular needs of particular groups (such as specific needs to comply with the Children Act)

It is unproductive to ask the architect to respond to a wishlist, that is to design for what might happen but equally might

---

19 Maggie Durran, *Making Church Buildings Work*, Canterbury Press, 2005.

not. I had a church being asked to consider installing child-size toilets as a nursery had expressed an interest in being in the building. To meet the requirements of the Children Act these would have been for the sole use of the nursery and would have cost a great deal to install. In the event the nursery fell through and such expense would have been a waste. A major adaptation should only be designed (this costs the architect's time) and later constructed if the lease or contract has already been signed with the prospective tenant. Similarly some churches have designed toilet facilities as if the maximum numbers in the building are the regular numbers. So there are toilets far in excess of real need. Many churches, even those holding occasional large events, can manage with a single disabled-accessible toilet; an occasional queue is not really any issue. It is far worse to use valuable space creating toilets that are almost never used. For an occasional major event it is possible to hire toilets for inside or outside the building. I know more than one church with a 'portaloo' in a corner of the crypt, and one had a temporary toilet in the vicarage garden for a one-off summer event.

The design ideas with which the architect responds will be refined and developed through this phase of the Development Cycle as firmer partnerships are formed and actual groups sign up to use the facilities.

Agree with the architect the kind of schedule the team wishes to follow. The architect knows what areas are still under discussion and what is firm, and over the months of formulating agreements with potential partners, user groups and tenants, the architect will help with considering the physical implications for the building.

The team and the architect will discuss what is needed in the design feasibility study, that is ensuring that the facilities wanted can be fitted appropriately into the space available and that the cost will be realistic. For projects that are likely to be complex or cost more that £50,000 it is advisable to employ a quantity surveyor early on so that the cost implications can be part of the perspective. One church was negotiating to bring in a government-funded youth project and had become very committed to that being the only way forward for regeneration. The government agency had a budget of £800,000 for capital works to add to the project but the first estimate for the cost of alterations to bring in the youth programme in a complex building intervention was £1,800,000. It is often more expensive to make major alterations to an existing building than to build a new one! In fact the budget could not be reduced by a significant amount because of the cost of installing a new floor with stairs and lifts. Explore whether proposed building alterations can realistically attract grants. A more modest scheme may fulfil most of what is wanted and cost far less and therefore more readily attract funds.

When the architect begins to produce outline ideas for the building, this is not an end-product, but the beginning of dialogue. Discuss the style of the design, how it will look and fit into the existing building. Discuss how the design meets the needs for facilities for the church's Strategy, but remember that it will be necessary to make some alterations later in the process. Discuss how the layout can and should work for circulating people. Discuss the potential cost and how to reduce it: simplify style, finishes and extent of provision, and consider the value of phased works.

This feasibility design takes time to develop and complete, and the major planning related to use and function should be resolved before the architect begins detailed design.

At an early stage agree with the architect the fees that will be incurred and at what point a contract should be signed. It is possible to pay the architect an hourly fee while feasibility work is being discussed, and a contract only comes into play when the church is ready to go ahead with a final form on the design. This can avoid the church being contractually obliged to pay percentage fees on work with which it decides not to go ahead.

Review notes on the building's *suitability to purpose* in the light of the feasibility work of the architect and the impact the potential community facilities will make on the style and quality of worship space and vice versa.

The feasibility stage with the architect is a dialogue in which the issues of alteration and addition and their suitability for existing and new uses must be discussed fully, so consider the impact of changes to:

- The approach to church for worship (look around)
- The sense of the church's ownership of its space
- The effect of visible intrusions on the integrity of space
- Respect for the story, history and architecture
- Respect for the future including reversibility of building alterations
- Can sound or silence be achieved when needed?
- Is liturgical movement, such as a procession, hampered or enhanced?
- Is there an impact on facilities for major festivals?
- Weddings, baptism and funerals: is there time and space and room for people to circulate?
- Are Children Act issues (toilets and security) sufficiently considered?[20]
- Have disability access and related issues been addressed adequately?
- Security of staff and users – alarm systems and other such issues – are they included?

This *suitability to purpose* has also to be considered from the other point of view, that of the tenant organization. Are the facilities needed easily accessible? Do we trip over church material, furniture or belongings or even their activity as we go about our business? Can children have safe unrestricted

---

20 If the church is going to run children's activities it must comply with every element of the Children Act. If the church is going to let its space to groups running children's programmes the physical space must be sympathetic or groups complying with the Act will not book the space. This may involve carefully locating toilets and ancillary facilities so that they can be used exclusively by only one group present in the building.

access to toilets? Can we access a servery close to where we are working where we can make refreshments? Is the entrance to the building easily visible so people can find their way to us? How much noise can we make and will we be interrupted by other people's noise?

For commercial space, such as offices, the suitability-to-purpose issues will be more comprehensive and the potential tenant will bring these issues to you, and the negotiations with outside groups that follow here will bring such issues to the fore.

It is not often that the solutions are impossible. After everyone has expressed their needs in detail the architect will look for creative ways to fit the essential ones, but some of the items may not be possible! During the negotiations the team can bear in mind that not everyone will get everything they want – even the church!

Tenants and construction

When the team is negotiating with potential long-term tenants there are several key factors to hold in mind about construction work. A tenant may wish for specific building works to be undertaken before they can use the space, requiring considerable capital investment. In one church I advised, a tenant had received a large grant to install lighting suitable for arts events. The grant in a clear sense belonged to the tenant and might not have been awarded to the church. I advised the church to only accept the installation of the lighting (which was sympathetic with the church refurbishment) if the construction once complete belonged to the church. This is an issue of risk. If the tenant were to go bankrupt (and it happens quite regularly in the arts sector) the creditors of the charity could claim all its assets to offset the debt; and this would include removing the lighting from the church and rendering the church almost unusable. This is a principle for all shared church buildings. The lease may in a careful legal framework become an asset of the charity or business; they may sell it on as part of a viable business, usually with the church having a right of veto on the next tenant, but no fixtures or fittings belong to the tenant and they may not be sold even if they are added by the tenant with the church's permission.

Another example is that when nurseries take on church space they often want to fit very tiny toilets, suitable to their use but not to others. I would recommend that no such toilets are fitted or the space is not usable by others if the nursery moves on. Alternatively, if child-sized toilets are fitted in a space at the tenant's expense then the tenant is obliged to replace them with adult-sized toilets when moving on. The significance is both ownership and use. Losing a significant tenant will create a hole in the cashflow, and if the need to refurbish toilets is added to the cost, and then time taken to replace them, it can be very difficult for the church.

Always seek legal advice when planning for medium- and long-term tenants, taking the outline arrangements to a diocesan lawyer for advice or getting legal advice from a lawyer in the charity sector. The eventual lease will need the approval of diocesan authorities when drawn up, so it is advisable to involve them in the nitty-gritty as terms are developed.

This is another of those areas where discussion with other churches with experience will help avoid the pitfalls!

Summary

Ensure all the functional issues and the layout of the altered building are suitable for the various uses before design begins.

The Strategy Report

Compile a Strategy Report, which will become the first section of the project's business plan, in the language of outsiders to whom you are going to negotiate further progress. It takes lots of material from the report to the church council.

The contents list will include most of the following:

1 Executive summary (one page at most)

2 Background to the regeneration project

This will include:

- statistical information on local issues, needs (details can be appended)
- results of local research and contacts made (details can be appended)
- information on local demand for provision and how this was identified.

3 The aim of the regeneration project (not of the church)

For example: St M's project will work with elderly local residents to provide programmes that encourage social activity and offer friendship and support.

4 Outcomes[21]

List your outcomes; these are the benefits or changes and effects that happen as a result of the project's activities.

A Big Lottery publication differentiates carefully between outcomes, outputs, inputs and long-term change.

Inputs are what is put into a project in order to deliver its outcomes or benefits. These are resources such as time, money and premises.

Outputs are the services and facilities that are delivered by the project and include such items as training courses, publications, lunches or advice sessions.

---

21 When the Lottery Community Fund has completed its transition into the Big Lottery its funding programmes will emphasize outcomes. A booklet is available from the Big Lottery, entitled *Your Project and its Outcomes*, by Sally Cupitt with Jean Ellis of Charities Evaluation Services.

The booklet quotes a case study:

Input >>	Output >>	Outcome >>	Long-term change
• staff • budget • venue • advertising	• one-to-one support • group work • outings	After using the project people will be more: • confident • aware of alternatives to being a young parent • ambitious • able toaccess training opportunities	There is less: • social exclusion • teenage pregnancy

If funding from the Big Lottery is going to be on the church's agenda for its regeneration project, either attend one of the workshops the Big Lottery are running to teach people how to approach fundraising geared to outcomes, or at least acquire one of their lists of outcomes they have funded in the past. This can identify many kinds of benefits of neighbourhood-based regeneration initiatives.

5 Ongoing activities

List the outputs. As the team begins to identify both need and demand, it is normally helpful to build up a programme of the likely activities that the regeneration initiative will provide. A schedule of activities on a weekly basis will enable the team to consider the extent of the planned programme and later (see pages 154ff.) its financial viability.

Visit another voluntary sector project that runs the type of programme the team is targeting as this will give a clearer idea of the depth of programme that is workable. In particular, if a project such as a social centre for the elderly is planned, creating a proposed programme and timetable of activities will test out whether the project occupies the surplus time that is available in the church or whether more and different activities can be added. The project for elderly people may run in the daytime but the evenings may still be available for children's programmes or for other art or education activity. Some space may be available for a more commercial letting.

6 Required inputs in order for activity to happen

How much building space or facilities, staff and management, money, building repair, finance need to be added to achieve the emerging Strategy? Is it really achieving the kinds of return the church wanted out of this?

Having produced a draft programme of activities, the team can now assess each of these inputs quite specifically. As far as possible, produce the assessments on spreadsheets or equivalent where items can be recalculated later as the business plan becomes more firm.

Expect this process to throw up lots of questions that the visits to interested potential partners in the external phase of Cycle Two may answer.

In a sense this is an iterative process that will become more specific and more fixed as the development process continues.

Present an initial view on the viability of the long term. Draft a revenue cashflow, including the costs of management and staff, use of building for whom and how often and the return from lettings. Be realistic and not over-optimistic by identifying optimum levels and then allowing for slow build-up and voids as you go along. While these details will change as you develop the plan, the structure will remain the same; the spreadsheet will allow you both to update and to see implications for the longer term. A simple budget and cashflow projection is included on page 154 to indicate some starting-points.

As a matter of good stewardship of the church's resources you should ensure that the whole concept of regenerating the church as a whole is met by the financial planning you produce. Will the church benefit from the investment of its building resources by becoming more able to undertake its mission? If the church has set out on a regeneration strategy because it is less than viable itself, probably financially as well as numerically, then the financial planning of the regeneration project must be seen to be addressing the church's need for viability, that is creating income that enables mission and growth to happen.

Plan letting rates for the extended use of the building, including for any initiatives on which the church is taking the lead, say the project for the elderly; outside funders will still accept that the project will need to pay its way in the building through a fee that covers rent and service charge.

7 *Risk analysis of the Strategy*

The team is now undertaking activities to consolidate the Strategy and the potential partnerships it is seeking to engage, based on earlier research. The risk analysis should now be updated and summarized for inclusion in the report on the Strategy.

Look particularly at all the inputs required and consider the risks involved in getting them in place.

Highlight areas of potential problem, from faculty and planning permission to capital funding.

Consider the staffing risks.

The letting risks may be best mitigated by planning to produce suitable policies, from health and safety to financial and letting procedures.

The value of highlighting these issues now is to inform the team of the many questions that can or will be resolved during further meetings with potential partners and with legal and planning advisers.

8 Option appraisal

Ensure that the Strategy fits with the work undertaken earlier on option appraisal and summarize the options appraisal in this report.

Summarize the feasibility dialogue with the architect and include this with your Strategy.

Summary

This Strategy Report informs the team as members now arrange to meet outside people again: those who will be direct beneficiaries, those who may be partners and those who may fund activity or building work. If you plan to hand out any of the written material in the report, stamp 'draft' on every page so the consolidation of research into strategy can easily be seen to be a step in the process and not cast in cement. It will ensure that people feel not marginalized or left out, but still free to come forward with ideas.

Research into potential funding

Research the possible sources

Few churches have all the money they need to make changes in their buildings to include new uses, either for the capital for altering the building or the revenue to keep community projects running. Researching potential outside funding early on enables the team to build in the funding constraints as a control on the extent of design or the kind of programmes that may be finally planned. For example, how much money is likely to come from outside sources, and from which ones, for altering the building?

Capital funding

Partnerships with the local authority or the regeneration board or the education authority for delivery of services may be accompanied by a package of money for capital works. Be sure to find out how much this is likely to be. Creating new facilities in listed buildings like churches is normally far more expensive per square metre than in a new building, so this figure is important to know.

Trusts' and foundations' levels of donations are researched in trust guides: books, data disks or online. Bear in mind that most can only fund 1 in 10 of the worthwhile applications they receive. After finding all those that might fund the project, and how much each gives to worthwhile projects, you could divide the total by 10, as on average this is what the church could receive.

The Landfill Tax scheme, if the church is in an eligible area, helps with money for community projects and with churches, but most seem to have a maximum grant of £25,000.

It is sometimes harder to assess the amount of money that can be raised from local sources so look at other churches and community projects in the area and ask them how much they managed to raise and how they did it. Do ask several, as any one of them could have done abnormally well or abnormally badly.

The resultant understanding of what may realistically be raised informs the dialogue with the architect. It is possible to design a good church hall, or hall facilities in a church, either for £500,000 or for £2,000,000. Functionally either could fulfil the task. The one the church gets is dependent on how much money you can raise. And whichever the church gets you will be seeking to meet the best possible combination of needs that you have identified in your research. Be mindful both in business planning and in design that you will get what you can afford, not your wildest dream.

Revenue funding

There are several ways to look at revenue funding as added facilities are planned.

Self-financing

Many church halls or community facilities in church, let at a fair rate, can earn enough money to pay for themselves. If every user, whether church or outside organization, pays a rent or letting fee, the income can be sufficient to cover all the costs. Maintaining a high level of bookings depends on being well managed and well cared-for.

Maintained through grants

Many community programmes and projects are sustained wholly by grants, and part of their fundraising will include money to pay for premises. If the church is to run any kind of full-time programme in the regenerated church, that programme would normally be able to raise money to pay its own way in the building. If the programme is for a group that church people would perceive as poor, it is not necessary to give that group a discount; groups that serve people from disadvantaged backgrounds are the most likely to get grant aid to help with their programmes and their costs.

Many local community centres or the local Council for the Voluntary Sector will be able to help in looking at this fundraising.

A hybrid scheme

It may be possible when considering the overall financial viability of the regeneration project to let some space commercially. A local estate agent or surveyor specializing in commercial property will be able to give an assessment of the rental value of space in the church. One church has the lower floor leased to a printing company and the upper floor continues as the church hall.

A tower room or unused vestry may be let as an office. In this case if the company is bringing in not much more than office furniture and a phone line, the lease can be shorter, and this leaves the church more flexibility for the future. Note, the status of leases on space in the church itself is currently under review. They should become easier to create, but it may be more difficult to get out of at a later stage. Consider the risks carefully and thoroughly.

It is possible to raise capital for community facilities in the church or hall regardless of whether the end-product will be self-financing or grant-dependent, as long as the case is fully explained in the business plan; that is that reasonable revenue projections are made based on realistic letting and booking rates or realistic levels of fundraising for grants.

Fundraising skills

If fundraising from outside bodies is needed then the team should identify someone with the time and skills to do the work. Skills in both verbal and written communication are important. This person will, with others of the team, need to meet researchers from the lottery or trusts when they visit and be able to clearly and succinctly answer questions from any part of the application material or the business plan. A comprehensive approach to fundraising can be found in *The UK Church Fundraising Handbook*.[22]

Summary

Raising outside funding is not easy, but there are significant funds available when the hard work is invested.

Capital from outside funders is dependent on presenting well-thought-out and well-managed, long-term sustainable projects.

Revenue may be raised from well-run premises or from ongoing grant-funding, but remember if you opt for the latter course you will have to keep a fundraising programme ongoing.

---

22 Maggie Durran, *The UK Church Fundraising Handbook*, Canterbury Press, 2003.

Consult

Stakeholder consultation

It is vitally important to the success of the regeneration of the church that the team keeps everyone with them. While the team is doing the detailed research and information gathering and forming opinions and recommendations, the aim is that everyone who has a stake in the church's future has access to the process and feels part of the decisions that are made. The team has an executive role on behalf of the church and the church council, but ultimately the regeneration project will not work if it is imposed on the church generally.

Consultation meetings should be set up to report on progress and present draft conclusions. But far more importantly, the team should be listening to ideas, questions, comments and criticisms from those present.

Hopefully the team's proposed Strategy for the way forward is now built on sound research and development. If people have questions then a team member can explain the process that led to the decision and the questioner will be able to understand the logic and think about it. Make a straightforward presentation, not too long, saving detail for question time and for handouts.

If the general mood of the consultation meeting is critical of plans, the team should not become angry or defensive but recognize that these are people with a serious concern for their church, and while all of them may not agree with careful work in explaining the project, they may become supporters.

Ask yourselves two questions.

Are those present convinced change has to happen?

No one likes change for its own sake. If there is an air of 'We'd rather stay as we are and why won't you let us?' it will be important to the long-term project that people are first reminded of the consequences of making no change. Revisit the numerical and financial issues.

Encourage a new look with a different starting-point. To work for a busy building to which many people are loyal and to which many people contribute financially is to invest in the future, not simply to tweak the present.

Are people convinced that the draft strategy from the team is the way forward?

Some of the people attending a stakeholder consultation meeting, even though they have accepted the need for change, will underneath still be hoping that nothing will happen or that a good fairy will come by with a magic wand. This may be expressed as a challenge to the team's leadership or competence in seeking a solution.

First, the team should not argue or become defensive out of their own fear that they are actually incompetent! We all have to deal with the fact that we don't know everything and we may not yet have the best solution. The team on the whole at this stage of the Development Cycle should be presenting the kinds of uses and programmes that will come into the church rather than a physical design (that comes later and may raise many more objections). People may be afraid of the incompatibility of various uses, and their reasons may be valid; they certainly deserve thought from the team and a reasoned response. If we have a youth group in the church, might their footballs damage the stained glass? A nursery has lots of equipment and furniture. Where will they put it when we need to use the hall? How can we have a place for quiet prayer for people who drop in if all this noisy activity is happening? All these comments and questions can be collected up and included in the dialogue with the architect. Reassure people that the team will bring information back to them, and then the administrator on the team can make sure this is done.

If people are registering big reactions to the development – negative that is – then it is better to have more consultation meetings than fewer. When people feel their voices have been heard they are far more likely to become supporters.

Don't be afraid to call in archdeacons and others as supporters of the project to hear both sides and help bring a harmonious conclusion.

Summary

Internal commitment is the bottom line of the foundation; if there are serious dissenters, hold more consultation events, not fewer.

Outside consultation

During the first round of outside visits the team will probably have found several possible options for partnership that have helped in formulating the Strategy. Each major proposal will have implications for the church's organization and Strategy. There are in fact so many creative possibilities that may have begun to form that this section can only run through some forms of partnership that other churches have developed and the ways they worked them out.

With each organization that is a potential partner an individual detailed development plan will be prepared. Team members will have in mind (or to hand) the various reports and elements that will impact in both directions positively and negatively for both church and partner and negotiate agreeable compromises that allow forward movement.

Each church will select the potential partners who expressed interest, and those for whom the chosen Strategy has implications, and map out second visits.

The meetings can be expected to include the path the church has chosen to go and a simple explanation of why. This is the point at which having turned the Strategy into everyday language rather than religious language comes into play. Identify the interest the potential partner indicated previously and use it as a stepping-off point to explore the potential for engagement in developing a common strategy.

While every partner may involve different conversations and negotiations, one key to success is to avoid closing a conversation on disagreement, especially disagreement that appears to be impossible to solve. At the end of each meeting sum up the areas of agreements and put disagreements onto the agenda of the next meeting. Churches seem often to lose out at this point, perhaps because they are inexperienced at negotiation. The potential tenant for example may suggest a rent that is far lower than the church wants to accept – every worthwhile commercial tenant will do this – but the church should state its determined rent level and hold to it. Keep the conversation going; do not give in, though eventually the church may want to concede a very small amount! Rent levels, especially for any kind of commercial use, especially if a large space is being considered, may be calculated by a commercial property surveyor agreeable to both parties. The surveyor will understand the many local factors that impact on the proposed rent and recommend a level that is reasonable to both parties. If the rent level (apart from the service charge) is less than the church would earn by selling its space, banking the money and earning interest, it is not worth renting out space. Too many churches fold up in the negotiation stage and effectively give away space at nominal rents and under terrible leases; this is bad stewardship of resources, especially for a church that is struggling and needs to renew itself on all fronts.

Once general agreement to proceed is agreed, the issues to address in follow-up visits include:

- Financial issues: for leases and letting, rent and service charges need to reach general agreement.
- Financial viability: each incoming group, organization or project must be financially sound if the church is going to have a medium- to long-term arrangement with them.
- Lease terms to be agreed.
- Letting arrangements to be worked out for regular letting (see *Making Church Buildings Work* for outline letting policies and booking forms).

- Agreements if capital works are required for the incoming tenant or by the church themselves before the tenant can come in.
- Timescales: can the time at which church space can be available synchronize with the need for space of the potential tenant?

Community projects may be planned, whether as a church initiative, or as a joint initiative with another local charity or with a local charity wishing to locate its activity in the church. The community project may be looking for sole-use space (that is no one uses that space when the project closes for the day); it may be happy with space that is used by others at other times of the week; it may require, for example under the Children Act, that it has sole use of some facilities when it is in the building. In each case there is a financial implication to be considered as rent and service charges are considered.

When rent (rather than letting costs, which are explored on page 153) is being considered, bear in mind the following points:

1 Rent is the proper return to its owner from the use of an asset, that is similar to the interest from a bank account. It is the amount the owner of the asset receives after all costs have been met. On the bank account this is the interest received after all charges have been deducted. Good stewardship requires that the church receives rent from its leased property, not just costs.

2 A service charge can be identified and added to the rent, rather than incorporated in a general sum. This charge covers any expenses the church continues to pay that are of benefit to the tenant. This is usually the structure used for costs in a shared building and covers such items as:
  (a) Building insurance, but not contents insurance
  (b) Management of the building
  (c) Cleaning and caretaking common public areas
  (d) Utilities, in proportion to building use by various tenants

(e) Maintenance and repairs

(f) Security

(g) Other attributable costs particular to each church.

The elements of the service charge as well as the rent will be part of the detailed discussion through which the church and the potential tenant discover whether the tenancy will work. Service charges change from time to time with the repair and running costs of the building and are open to the scrutiny of the tenant, but the rent will be predetermined in the lease.

3 Access. Most tenants taking on a lease will want to access their activity space at any time. If there are limitations that really are unavoidable then the church should raise these for discussion early on. The entrance may also be used on a weekday for an occasional funeral or on weekends for weddings, so business visitors would need to enter through the crowd. Church festivals may include midnight at Christmas and dawn at Easter, Good Friday and other weekdays. This may impact on the activity of the tenant.

4 Noise. Are there times when noise from a tenant's activity would be unacceptable? And vice versa, would the noise of services or organ practice or bell ringers be impossible for the tenant?

5 Shared space. Set out the guidelines on how common space and circulation space may be used. Can anyone put out display stands (if health and safety allows them)? Can anyone put posters or information on the walls (church or tenant)? What items can be placed or stored temporarily or permanently in common space? What will be the arrangements for and rules governing disposal of rubbish? Should either tenant or church be advised if the other is holding a significant event that may dominate circulation space?

6 Toilets. These may be located in common space and used by all tenants and the church. Arrangements for access may be varied. When the church is used for a public event all sorts of people coming straight off the street may be in the

toilets, and this may be impossible for some tenants, such as those working with children. Standards of cleanliness and responsibility for it should be agreed. When the church is open to the public for just dropping in, toilets may be accessible only by key.

These items are usually gathered under the reference of Heads of Terms.

For setting up letting programmes on church space, general agreement from church authorities should be sought. Normally each non-religious event held in church (not the hall) should have faculty, but for a church that is seeking to get activity going every day this is not possible. A general agreement giving permission for a variety of activities within reasonable limitations can be given by the authorities concerned.

At present consecrated church buildings may not be subject to leases, though an Act of Parliament is being discussed that would allow leases on minority spaces. If a major space is to be let out for other than religious activity, it is normal to seek redundancy (which places the building in the control of the diocese) and then the minor space that will continue as a place of worship is consecrated as a licensed worship area. This course of action changes the faculty status and it is best to have a conversation with the secretary of the Diocesan Advisory Committee and Archdeacons on the particular implications. For example, if all the furniture and contents of the church space were covered by faculty, the tenants would not want to apply for faculty before moving their desks or bringing in a bookshelf! Redundancy solves this problem.

Summary

Place a comprehensive understanding of the needs of potential user groups or tenants alongside the needs of the church and its ongoing mission. Resolve the differences, finding a third way where necessary.

Revisiting local people

Local people are consulted to keep them up to date with the development programme and encourage them to 'own' it with the church.

Local residents are incredibly important to the church's Strategy for regeneration. Local people are the target of re-engagement; they may be the clients of community projects, audience at the music events, the dancers at the pensioners' tea dance. So keep them onside. It's a great discipline to reduce the whole Strategy and the reasons for it to a dozen slides on PowerPoint with limited associated notes. Being able to identify the fundamental skeleton of the project will enable the team to have a variety of conversations with people while not straying from the essentials of the Strategy.

Since the Strategy is getting beyond the Preferred Option and approaching detailed planning, hold a new event for local residents that enables them to hear the results of the church's research and a little about the Strategy. Avoid mentioning organizations and departments with whom the church as yet have no agreement, but refer in general terms to outcomes the church is targeting. For example, 'Our research showed that there is shortage of provision for social gatherings for elderly people and help for some who need more support, so we are looking for a partnership to provide daily programmes of activities for pensioners.' Or, 'We realize there are a large number of children in our area with working parents, so we want to target partnerships in providing after-school care till parents finish work.' Or, 'There are many families in our neighbourhood for whom English is a second language and we would like to run programmes to help parents understand the children's homework so they can support them.'

Those attending the consultation may offer suggestions for partnership or even connections that will facilitate them. At such events I have even met trustees from charities – they all live in someone's church neighbourhood or parish – who have recommended applying to their trusts for grants to help get going!

If the architect has prepared the feasibility plan in time, her or his outline plan may be displayed and become part of the consultation. Activity groups, from scouts to aerobics teachers, may turn up to see how things might go and have important suggestions to make. Where one church hall was to be completely rebuilt, one couple looking at the plans offered to put the wooden floor of the old hall to use in a house renovation!

When local people are drawn in at a creative level in the development, just like church members, they will increase their sense of ownership and are more likely to join in fundraising activity and to gain a sense of achievement when the work is complete.

The church's applications for faculty and for planning permission will all be pinned to the church gate to invite local comment or objection. A creative relationship in the development stage will get a good hearing when problems are raised, and will result in fewer objections to be overcome.

Summary

The parish is the place where this renewed activity by the church is focused, so get engaged with local people, residents and businesses. Establish common ground through new and determined relationships.

Revisiting the local authority

Once the church has a Strategy set up with target activities in its regeneration, the visits to local authority departments will rapidly become more focused. General interest at senior officer levels may now be channelled to departments where action can happen. (Sometimes passing you along the line covers up disinterest, so be careful of your time and that you are not being passed to someone who has no power in the system!)

Some church and local authority partnerships have included:

Rebuilding a three-storey church hall at the council's expense, taking the lower floors for a *social services* initiative with homeless people. The upper floor was returned to the church as a fully refurbished hall for its church and community activity, along with a sizeable lump sum. Negotiation and communication are still important between church and tenant because they share the one building and there are management issues to address. The lease is for 125 years, but the church received all it wanted in return for rebuilding a semi-derelict building.

Small *start-up businesses* supported by the council and regeneration partners occupy office space in a church roof.

A local authority and trust partnership is creating business space for small businesses, creating new structure that will occupy a large part of the underused nave. This will provide everyday occupancy and leave additional space for use for community activity alongside the licensed worship area at the east end.

Many churches have provided the space and local authorities the programmes in initiatives to tackle *unemployment*. Various directorates may initiate such programmes and be seeking suitable town centre space.

Education departments have often been the funding partners of youth programmes, whether youth clubs or targeted group work. Schools and churches (not only church schools) often co-operate to provide programmes, from pre-school provision to after-school and homework clubs. Saturday schools are often run by ethnic minority groups with a concern for their own children and may be seeking space.

For church development initiatives that fall within the remit of *European Social Funding*, a partnership with the local authority for match-funding is normally required. It is preferable to find the appropriate department within the local authority and gain their support before applying to Europe. The council may refuse to match European funding unless they have been part of developing a plan which meets some of their own objectives for the neighbourhood.

The council's department for community development may be of assistance. Sometimes, however, this department is a low-level, low-budget arm of a larger directorate and has little power or effect. They may use their funding to support a local Council for the Voluntary Sector (CVS) and even distribute funds through the CVS. One church running a day centre for the elderly, including those with mental illness such as Alzheimer's, gets its director's salary from such a fund.

Visit any department with whom the team's initial conversation suggested there was potential. Update key officers and councillors on the strategy the church is now following and on partnerships the church is seeking. Allow the conversation to be very flexible, as the department may be interested, but wish for a different format and basis for partnership. In urban centres councils at times have projects they wish to create, say through social services, that are waiting for suitable premises. At times also councils may be preparing bids for regional funding and may wish to adapt some elements of your plan so that the church becomes a point for delivery of a local project. Engage in a dialogue that leads into a more formal partnership.

There will be people who were keen on the church becoming active in its community but who made no specific suggestions at the time. Set up communication reminders to keep people advised; the link may be very useful as you progress, and they may still be on your side when council debates happen.

Remember too that when local or national government is involved in the local provision they are accountable on a number of fronts for spending public money:

- Equal Opportunities matters a great deal. Public money must benefit all local people without discrimination. If your church is unable to offer services without discrimination then progress may be hampered. Discuss the issues in the church by writing your own equal opportunities statement and policy before it is required. One local church was turned down by its local authority as it did not offer equality for women – the church would not accept women priests. Prepare for questions and potential issues.
- Councils will be concerned about local voters, so your consultation with local residents and their engagement in the process of development will be important.
- Councils have to meet comprehensive objectives in targeting key disadvantaged groups, and therefore any partnership will involve good monitoring and review processes to ensure targets are being met.
- Council spending is audited by the national audit office of central government to ensure all is in order. Spending through partnership with the church will be subject to such scrutiny, particularly for larger sums.

Summary

Local authorities, from councils to health authorities, are set up to benefit local people and for the common good. Working with them involves the church in 'loving our neighbours as ourselves' and working with them even when they are not people who are like us.

Revisiting regeneration agencies

Regeneration agencies are set up with boards of directors or trustees to ensure that the objectives of the funding body, national, regional or local government, are met in the way money is invested in local initiatives. Local business people and community leaders are often on such boards, and staff often have had experience of working for regional and local government.

Boards and staff of any one regeneration agency may operate in a very different way from the next one; it depends on the people involved. The regeneration agency will function as the distributor of funding to invest in a strategy for regeneration and will be looking at the overall picture of need in an area. The church may find it can be a partner and deliver services for local people that might not be the church's first choice. The regeneration agency may be wanting to place an employment training project or provision for work with families while the church had first identified the needs of children.

It is important for the church team to discover exactly what the regeneration agency is wanting to achieve and how it wants to achieve it, and then to look for synchronicity or common interests – a win–win.

Develop the relationship with officers, who are normally able to help shape the application that is made for funding. Keep in touch. It may also be helpful to be in contact with board members. If any of you know any board members, ensure they are well briefed about your Strategy and your application so that when an application is put forward for inclusion in the budget more members know what the church is trying to achieve and can support you.

Application processes with regeneration agencies are always long and complicated! They are full of the language and concepts of government departments and geared to their needs, not those of the applicant. Review the notes on page 146 on language before you start. Be especially careful not to use religious language, and where the church's provision will be for local people regardless of religion, say so by using the phrase 'local community provision'. Update the Option Appraisal if you haven't already done so as this uses the language that is required by the government sector. The local Council for the

Voluntary Sector is likely to be able to offer help with this form-filling or have contacts who can. It can be very hard to grasp what the questioner is asking without some clues from someone in the know!

Regeneration agencies often have a small staff who are quite entrepreneurial. Invite key officers to the church's consultation events, the launch of the Strategy and other events in this development programme as they may notice an opportunity for the future by meeting local people with the church.

In the lifespan of a regeneration agency targets and objectives change from year to year. Staff change as well, and with new staff there may be new perspectives on how to deliver objectives. Keep communications open and there may be new opportunities for the church in future years.

Summary

Regeneration agencies are set up to make an injection of resources that effect change in a neighbourhood, area or region. Be prepared for delivering their objectives through your church, with their help only in the short-term.

Revisiting local groups

Revisit local voluntary sector groups who expressed interest in partnership and engage in further dialogue.

Factors to look out for

Many local charitable groups who are seeking premises or partnership do not work with long lead-in times. If the church is going to require major fundraising followed by major building alterations, small community organizations are normally not able to wait. So on long-term projects, indications of interest may not be turned into formal agreement until the building is almost ready to take them.

It is common for small local groups to overestimate their

own potential for expansion or ability to sustain a large project. Many small arts groups approached one church whose refurbishment included a theatre. Most were run by two or three people and had experience of occasional presentations; none had a business plan or bank references, yet each wanted to take on a lease on the theatre that would only be financially viable with a full programme of successful performances or with a high level of grant aid from the Arts Council. When asked for a business plan and assurances of funding, most groups disappeared, with a great deal of grumbling. Even the successful theatre company that took on the lease, with business plan and financial references in place, only managed to run for two years before becoming bankrupt.

Before leasing out parts of a large building development ensure the church's own business plan stands up to issues such as voids (when there are gaps in income as a result of gaps in letting). Ensure that the break-even point is tested for sensitivity when rates are set. If the church's viability depends on all spaces being let all the time, the project will fail as there are bound to be gaps from time to time.

Many local groups are very small and are seeking a meeting place, and a letting arrangement is in their best interest. Such groups will make indications of interest (backed up by a letter) but may have changed considerably by the time building alterations are complete. However, where you have received lots of expressions of interest there are bound to be others with an interest who take their place. On one major church refurbishment, we had 45 interested groups before we started, and when we opened after three years, we were fully booked, but none of the 45 took on space!

Voluntary groups very often expect the church to provide space at knock-down and unrealistic rates, and be less than businesslike in their agreements. Be straightforward from the start. Any community group for whom you would want to feel sorry – and give a knock-down rate – is very able to raise money from grants to pay their way. If they can't pay a basic fee, check out their credibility – they may not be well run!

Even the church's own parent and toddler group will be able to get grants for its occupation of church space.

Set out a clear written document or letter summarizing mutual understanding of the basis on which the group will be in the church. Churches are notorious for having all sorts of strange verbal agreements that seem controlling and non-negotiable at a later date. A written agreement that includes issues such as letting rates rising annually with inflation; scope for regular bookings to be made up to three months in advance; and other basic agreements that protect the church's interests in the future, should all be included. If someone does have free or discounted space, make that discretionary and time-limited so that if circumstances change the church may change the arrangement.

Get diocesan legal advice on how the church is setting up lettings, or leases in the case of church property other than the church, because it is important to ensure that a letting cannot by mistake be turned into a tenancy. For example, it is not wise to allow a group, except under a formal tenancy, to have sole-use locked space – for example a storage cupboard to which the church does not have a key – as this may create a tenancy! Get the rules right to protect the church in years to come.

There are many commercial groups such as private nurseries, health and leisure groups and others looking for space to hire. They are commercial in their operation even though they serve local people and local communities. Ensure that the arrangements are professionally drawn up.

Do not let anyone use the space until the church has a legal agreement with them, or you may by default enter into an agreement that the church would not want. A simple booking form[23] may be used, while a more long-term arrangement is being prepared.

Avoid being so grateful or relieved when a seemingly good tenant has approached the church that you give them a wildly

---

23 See *Purple Pack* from Southwark Diocese, or *Making Church Buildings Work* (see n. 19).

unrealistic agreement. This is a good reason for preparing your financial projections before the church makes agreements. Good tenants will not go away while the church negotiates properly if they are a reliable and worthwhile group.

Summary

Many voluntary sector groups function just like churches and often struggle to survive. Be careful not to get drawn into their problems; deal with your own first and later you may as a successful local partner be able to offer more assistance. Don't be hurried into ill-thought-out arrangements by the pressure from small struggling groups.

Ensure that all your agreements are based on proper safe legal groundwork. And remember that a lot of the best local partnerships with churches are with local charities and welfare agencies.

Review

When outside partners and others interested in the development have more fully committed themselves, and the shape of their engagement is clearer, the team can now formulate the elements of the application of the Strategy. At this stage in the development cycle, several pieces of drafting and research can happen that will enable the team and subsequently the church council and members to be sure that the project is viable and sustainable and that the risks have been fully identified and action planned to minimize the effects.

SWOT analysis development

Update the SWOT analysis that was first prepared on the flipchart pages and add to the team's Strategy as an A4 sheet. This summary will become part of your business plan so turn the language into that used by secular organizations. This may involve making it less personal and using phrases such as 'outside the religious purposes of the charity'. Change the names of roles to ones that outsiders understand.[24]

Church	>	faith group
	>	charity
Vicar	>	chairperson
PCC	>	church council
	>	management committee
	>	trustees
Parish	>	council ward

The SWOT analysis should now focus clearly on the chosen Strategy. For example, if the selected strategy is to create partnerships to develop a social centre for pensioners under STRENGTHS the team can emphasize the particular skills and experience that people in the church have to bring to the chosen strategy. Under OPPORTUNITIES include the results of the demographic research and any identified local lack of facilities. This will include the numbers of pensioners living in the area, the number of centres and facilities providing for their needs, and the identified demand for more provision. Similarly, the potential partnerships identified in Cycle One should now feature in the OPPORTUNITIES, and if outside authorities suggested some constraints these go in THREATS.

Summary

Review all reports and paperwork and ensure it is in the language of non-church people. Get help if necessary.

Management of the regeneration project

This management, and the two reports which follow – the financial plans and the draft business plan – should be a prime

---

24 Further work on language and outside organizations and potential funders is in *The UK Church Fundraising Handbook* (see n. 22).

opportunity to test and prove the viability of the strategy for regeneration at the level of the resources required to make it happen. Raising money for the construction of new facilities is only a beginning and no plans should be made for such physical alterations unless it can be shown that the resultant project can be well run and well maintained and definitely can produce the outcomes that are built into the Strategy. Outside funders will always want pragmatic reassurance that the project is viable before they will invest capital in its creation. What are the issues to address?

Bookings and lettings

A well-used and busy building will need a process for letting. Enquiries will come into someone's desk on a booking form and need to be processed: letting times and access times agreed, letting fee agreed, deposit collected and banked, arrangements for someone to unlock and close afterwards and so on.

A package of material that includes sample booking forms can be found in *Making Church Buildings Work*.[25]

Rules for those who use the building

A handbook is helpful in giving rules for health and safety and to define limits and agreements. Some churches manage with a sheet of rules handed to each person when they are booking the space.

Always use a system of deposits so that everyone booking the space makes a deposit that can be used to cover any breakage or damage that they cause.

People should also know that certain inappropriate behaviour, such as overstaying, rudeness to the caretaker or other staff, damage, or upsetting the neighbours with noise, will result in them being refused any future bookings.

---

25 *Making Church Buildings Work* (see n. 19).

If the regeneration project will involve long-term lettings such as to a nursery or project for the elderly, a different agreement should be drawn up about care of the building. The agreement should be clear about who is responsible for cleanliness before and after the group's sessions; who is the link person with the church; what may be stored in the church or hall and where and when; what may be left in the fridge, and so on. What is the church's expectation of the space being clear after every session? These are important, as a group that uses the building every day will begin to feel at home enough to adapt things to suit themselves without due regard for others using the building on the evenings and weekends. In the early days of use it will be important to insist that the required standard is maintained.

Maintenance

Only a well-maintained building will be in demand all the time, even when good maintenance standards cost more and cause the letting rate to be higher.

Plan a maintenance programme for the building. The architect can give an estimation of the lifecycle of fixtures and fittings and can give an estimate of how long the cycle will be before, for example, redecoration is necessary and toilets will need replacement. This information with be useful when looking at the financial planning.

Consider the internal finishes and their maintenance. A woodblock floor will probably need major cleaning and re-varnishing once each year and the premises kept closed for a few days while this is done. At the same time work may be done to upgrade or repair other facilities. This leads to the conclusion that it is useful to have a week or two each year with no bookings so the building can catch up.

How often will the busy church building need thorough cleaning? If a nursery is to use the space every weekday, the floor may need washing every day before they arrive. Toilets should be cleaned every day if the space is used every day. And in a busy building it is worth asking the architect to design in facilities in the toilets and kitchen that lend themselves to thorough cleaning and hard wear, for example, tiles on the floor and walls so all smells can be washed away easily. Employing a cleaner to work early every day may be necessary as well as asking groups to leave the space clean for the next group to come in.

Conservation

When a Grade I or Grade II* building is being adapted for additional uses it is helpful to have a professionally drawn up conservation plan, usually prepared by an architect or surveyor with appropriate skills.

In the plan, every element of the building will be considered, key points about it stated and issues to do with its care addressed. How should the church care for the woodblock floor, the polished pews and other features? What cleaning methods and materials can safely be used? For example, specify what polish can be used on the woodwork and instruct that the Victorian tile floor should be brushed not washed, and outline the care to be taken of fabrics.

The plan will address repair issues also and elements that should be identified and protected when building alterations are considered – that could be anything from memorials to medieval walls.

Once expert advice has been acquired, make sure the cleaner and others who care for the building know what the expert has said.

Premises management

A busy building needs management. Plans will be needed for times to clean, procedures for getting minor repairs done, disputes over keys or times or groups over-running. Do not expect the vicar to do this work on top of their own existing job.

When groups are in during the evening someone will be needed to lock up, to ensure that bins and flammable rubbish have been put outside and to set security alarms.

The lettings procedures and policies will require management and recommendations made to the committee when change is needed.

Staff

Make an estimate of the tasks needed above and the time needed to complete them and begin to form up a list of staffing requirements. It is unlikely that all the tasks can be done by one person, especially if the building will be used seven days each week.

For cleaning, it could be a part-time cleaner working five mornings, but if seven days are really needed, a contract cleaning company may be the best option as they can allocate different staff on different days.

A full-time job may be needed for the caretaking, to cover all the out-of-hours locking and checking.

It is very unlikely that either the cleaner or the caretaker will have all the skills for management and administration, but many churches have a part-time manager or administrator.

For the budget in the next chapter, this work will need to be priced. Use the local paper to see the job descriptions and pay rates for similar work and set your levels.

'Hall' committee

Just as many churches have a separate hall committee, the best way forward for the regenerated church may be to have a management committee in addition to the church council. This committee will concern itself with the setting up and management of the new facility, leaving the church council free to get on with its primary focus on the religious activity of the church.

People with practical skills and experience with community projects can be recruited for the committee. The church council may form this as a sub-committee of the church council and establish its terms of reference. The committee should get its annual budget approved by the church council.

The committee can meet before the project is under way to set up the guidelines for the way forward. Policies and procedures for the following are essential.

- Financial planning and management
- Health and safety
- Children Act
- Security and safety of staff and those who use the building
- Letting handbook, booking and deposit policies
- Staff appointment procedures and appraisal
- Equal opportunities policy and procedures
- Consultation with people who use the building regularly
- Administration
- Caretaking and cleaning

The committee should expect to review the financial situation at every meeting.

Summary

Prepare a handbook or other written agreement of terms and conditions of use.

Prepare to employ staff for a busy and well-cared-for building, as only a well-cared-for building will stay busy and effective in the infrastructure of local life.

Financial planning

Most churches have thorough financial reporting, but few have developed financial planning and many do not have an annual budget. At the foundation of the regeneration strategy for the church there should be a system of thorough financial planning and budgeting. Most major funders will also require cashflow projections. Whether or not the church is going to need to account for itself to outside funders, the management of money should be more sophisticated when busy everyday use of the church is planned. Staff will be appointed and the church should know it will have the money in place to pay them. If deposits are being taken on lettings, then that money does not belong to the church until the date of the booking so cashflow must be carefully checked. In fact, it quickly becomes obvious that forward planning of finance is essential to good management.

Letting rates and income

Using a projected schedule of use and projected letting rates a sum can be arrived at.

A church has set two letting rates for its hall, £15 per hour for children's groups and small groups and £25 per hour for adults and larger groups. Bookings such as wedding receptions and parties at the weekend are £750 per day.

The schedule of use at present is shown in the figure on page 153. When combined with the letting rates this gives projected income. The figure on page 154 shows a simple budget for this community hall. I will run through every line then show a cashflow projection over several years. Create a table (in Excel or Lotus 123) so that the budget can be updated as the church's planning proceeds.

Notes about the budget are given here. For planning the church regeneration project, a similar rationale or justification should be available for every line of the projection, ensuring that planning is financially realistic.

1 *Lettings income.* The projected lettings income of the community space is calculated by creating the projected schedule and multiplying it appropriately by the letting rates.

Hourly Rates

	weekday up to 15 in group	weekday over 15 in group	weekend all users	
adults	£ 25	£ 35	£ 35	per hour
children	£ 15	£ 25	£ 35	per hour

rate	Monday	Tuesday	Wednesday	Thursday	Friday	Saturday	Sunday
child hours: L							
H	11	5	8	13	9		6
adult: L	3	5	3	3	3		
H	6	6	9	6	6	7	
	£390	£350	£420	£270	£360	£245	£210

per week	£2,245
per year	£114,495

Part 2: The Development Cycle

	2006	2007	2008	2009
Income				
Lettings	£90,000	£120,000	£120,000	£ 120,000
Expenditure				
Administrator	£15,000	£15,000	£15,000	£15,000
Cleaner	£7,000	£7,000	£7,000	£7,000
Caretaker	£7,000	£7,000	£7,000	£7,000
Heat	£4,000	£4,000	£4,000	£4,000
Light	£2,000	£2,000	£2,000	£2,000
Office costs	£3,000	£3,000	£3,000	£3,000
Phone	£1,000	£1,000	£1,000	£1,000
Stationery	£300	£300	£300	£300
Maintenance	£3,000	£3,000	£3,000	£3,000
Rent	£15,000	£35,000	£35,000	£35,000
Publicity	£1,000	£200	£200	£200
Cleaning materials	£2,000	£2,000	£2,000	£2,000
Minor repairs	£5,000	£5,000	£5,000	£5,000
Supplies	£1,000	£1,000	£1,000	£1,000
Major repairs fund	£15,000	£15,000	£15,000	£15,000
Insurance	£ 7,000	£ 7,000	£ 7,000	£ 7,000
Equipment	£2,000	£2,000	£2,000	£2,000
Total	£90,300	£90,300	£109,500	£109,500
Opening balance	0	−£300	£29,400	£39,900
Closing balance	−£300	£29,400	£39,900	£50,400

Note: Inflation is not included

2 *Administrator.* A busy programme will require dedicated staff time to ensure that everything runs smoothly and is well co-ordinated. The figure in my budget is for an administrator 25 hours each week at the going rate in my local paper. The hours have been calculated by determining that most callers about the hall facilities come between 10am and 3pm. Outside of those hours staff on duty, such as the caretaker, have booking enquiry forms that can be passed to the administrator for processing.[26] Ensure that the total in the budget includes the employer's National Insurance payment and pension.

3 *Cleaner.* Busy premises need regular – even daily – cleaning. Budget for a cleaner on just above minimum wage or again check the local newspaper advertisements. (The same amount may be spent on a cleaning contract with an agency.) Include the percentage for National Insurance.

4 *Caretaker.* Premises that are open morning to night need a caretaker to do out-of-hours access and locking up at night. This will be a full-time job with an agreement of what hours will be worked in total each week. Time off each week should be agreed and holiday cover allowed for in the budget. The 35-hour week salary + cover for days off and holidays + National Insurance contribute to this budget figure.

5 *Heat and light.* For new facilities with new heating equipment the engineer will be able to give the team an assessment of its running cost for heat and light. For premises with an old system that is now going to run every day, multiply up the existing average costs.

6 *Water rates* may be estimated as a multiple of present costs.

7 *Office costs.* Setting up an office for the administrator has an initial high cost that includes the computer, furniture

---

26 Much more information on administrators for community projects is available in *Making Church Buildings Work* (see n. 19).

and other equipment.[27] Annual costs include updated equipment and materials.

8 *Phone.* Once set up, the phone may be busy. It must have an answering facility for out-of-hours enquiries. Take the projected cost from either the church office or similar centres in the area.

9 *Stationery.* Notices, letters, booking forms, mailings. Set a figure for purchasing everything basic to get started, and set an annual figure from a comparison with church use or based on another centre.

10 *Maintenance.* The best way to set a maintenance budget is to discuss costs with the team that designs the facilities. This includes a lift maintenance contract, without which the church cannot operate a lift, fire equipment and alarms systems, all moveable equipment, regular care programmes for floors and finishes throughout, and any other items that the architect may suggest. A church with a flat roof may need to budget for refinishing it every few years. Doors, window frames and fences will need repainting every three to five years.

11 *Minor repairs.* While the actual amount spent each year will fluctuate wildly, this budget figure should cover all minor repairs, from pipes and taps to broken windows and door handles. Set a figure by using an average of the previous three years' figures.

12 *Major repairs fund.* All busy facilities will require upgrading works every few years. Every five to seven years for toilets and tiles, to every fifteen years for electrical wiring and circuits. Eventually roofs will need replacing. This figure is almost never taken seriously by churches, who fail to budget for it, but this sum should be reserved in an account for this purpose only, so that facilities can be upgraded with passing years to maintain a very high standard. The figure can be calculated by getting specific details of the lifespan of fittings and materials from the architect and creating a

---

27 Of course, the figure would be much lower if you purchase second-hand furniture.

projection of when each will need replacing and what savings should be made to cover that cost. Calculate by using current costs, but each year increase by inflation the amount calculated to be set aside in that and subsequent years.

13 *Rent*, payable to the church. The use of church facilities by other groups and local people can be paid for in the accounts through rent. Set the rate by considering the value of the space if let to one user for the entire time. Alternatively set the rate by deciding what can be afforded after money is set aside for repairs and maintenance. There should always be a payment made (even if the church returns it to the regeneration project as a donation), as it represents good stewardship by the church of its assets and a clear sense of due responsibility by the project.

14 *Publicity.* Allowing access for all local people to the church facilities is only possible if everyone knows about it. Budget for mailings, leafleting, advertisements in the local paper or other forms of promotion.

15 *Cleaning supplies.* My figure comes from a church that has up to 10,000 people each week in its building. Your church will probably have fewer! But everything from toilet rolls to mops and buckets that are needed by the cleaners are included.

16 *Insurance.* A building used every day is going to have a higher insurance bill than one used on Sundays only. This figure can be readily set by consulting the church's insurers and getting a new quote.

17 *Equipment.* After an initial larger cost for chairs and tables and other essentials, the budget each year will need to allow for replacement of worn-out or damaged equipment. Ensure that equipment is not left in a deteriorated state or, again, lettings will drop. It may be necessary every ten years or so to write off all existing equipment and purchase new. Set the budget to allow for this.

18 *Miscellaneous.* This always gets used but should only include tiny items. If a new category seems to recur make it a proper budget item.

19 *Opening balance*. What the project had in the bank at the beginning of the year.

What the project has in the bank at the end of the year is profit. In reality the savings account should also hold the major repairs fund and the surplus on the minor repairs fund. Profit need not be high or significant, but a loss here is a problem. If the end-of-year balance looks as if it will be negative, first look at the income and ensure that letting rates are realistically and responsibly set. The expenditures outlined here are the basics for running a good community facility. If the deficit does not occur in future years (here I have projected four years), then it may be possible in the setting-up year to set aside less savings for repairs, but to do the same in successive years is counterproductive: address the letting rates as the means of the project paying its way.

Monthly cashflow projection

Some funders require a monthly cashflow projection (see Figure 8.3). It gives a more detailed picture than the annual budget, and several issues can be highlighted.

The key issues that can be identified in a monthly cashflow projection are the effects of quarterly and annual payments. While income will normally be fairly level throughout the year, expenses are not.

Figure 8.3 shows the cashflow spread out over a *typical* year of running. A number of expenses are the same each month. Others such as insurance and the maintenance contract for the lift are once each year. The utilities are quarterly. With a steady predictable level of income, the projections look fine and in this case I would recommend that the annual rent payable to the church increases.

However, look at the *first year* of the project in Figure 8.4. There are the same recurring costs, plus a number of opening costs, such as office costs, in buying the administration equipment, and the cost of furniture for the hall. Items like insurance have to be paid by the day of opening, and the result is that the bank balance at the bottom is a disaster. This is a challenge for the team. Every project when it starts will have a scenario of this kind and will need to find responsible ways to start, while never going into deficit.

Here are some possibilities for remedying this cashflow problem.

1 Arrange for the insurance and utilities to be paid by monthly standing order.
2 Additionally, I removed the saving for major repairs from the first year but was still left with a mid-year deficit of £17,000, although by the end of the year there is a tiny surplus.
3 What if the church loans the project working capital of £20,000 pounds for the year. In this case the project never goes into deficit and at the end of the year has more than £22,000 in the bank and can repay the working capital to the church. However, don't short-circuit the method: run the cashflow projection forward for at least another year with full costs, as the same working capital may still be needed.

On an ordinary budget (see pages 160–1) I might have anticipated (in the left-hand figures) that I would be OK because there was a surplus on the year overall. *Not* so.

In successive years, as the figure on pages 160–1 indicates, the income is consistently higher and can more than cover all costs including the savings for major repairs. All these financial issues will be the regular agenda items for the meetings of the management committee. For management it is preferable to set up a spreadsheet with a cashflow budget that rolls forward each month giving the actual expenditure for the past three months and the projected expenditure for the next twelve months; this allows the committee to see the bigger picture as they discuss detail.

Cashflow One: a general year

		January	February	March	April	May	June
Income							
Lettings	£120,000	10000	10000	10000	10000	10000	10000
TOTAL income		10000	10000	10000	10000	10000	10000
Expenditure							
Administrator	£ 15,000	1250	1250	1250	1250	1250	1250
Cleaner	£ 6,996	583	583	583	583	583	583
Caretaker	£ 6,996	583	583	583	583	583	583
Heat	£ 2,000			500			500
Light	£ 1,000			250			250
Office costs	£ 2,004	167	167	167	167	167	167
Phone	£ 800	200			200		
Stationery	£ 1,007	600	37	37	37	37	37
Maintenance	£ 1,500	1000				500	
Minor repairs	£ 504	42	42	42	42	42	42
Rent	£ 15,000	1250	1250	1250	1250	1250	1250
Publicity	£ 1,995	1500	45	45	45	45	45
Cleaning materials	£ 996	83	83	83	83	83	83
Major repairs fund	£ 15,000	1250	1250	1250	1250	1250	1250
Supplies	£ 504	42	42	42	42	42	42
Insurance	£ 7,000	7000					
Equipment	£ 3,991	2000	181	181	181	181	181
TOTAL expenditure	£82,293	17550	5513	6263	5713	6013	6263
Opening balance		8000	450	4937	8674	12961	16948
Closing balance		450	4937	8674	12961	16948	20685

July	August	September	October	November	December	January	February	March	April
10000	10000	10000	10000	10000	10000	10000	10000	10000	10000
10000	10000	10000	10000	10000	10000	10000	10000	10000	10000
1250	1250	1250	1250	1250	1250	1250	1250	1250	1250
583	583	583	583	583	583	583	583	583	583
583	583	583	583	583	583	583	583	583	583
		500			500			500	
		250			250			250	
167	167	167	167	167	167				
200			200			200			200
37	37	37	37	37	37	37	37	37	37
						1000			
42	42	42	42	42	42	42	42	42	42
1250	1250	1250	1250	1250	1250	1250	1250	1250	1250
45	45	45	45	45	45	45	45	45	45
83	83	83	83	83	83	83	83	83	83
1250	1250	1250	1250	1250	1250	1250	1250	1250	1250
42	42	42	42	42	42	42	42	42	42
					7000				
181	181	181	181	181	181	181	181	181	181
5713	5513	6263	5713	5513	6263	13546	5346	6096	5546
20685	24972	29459	33196	37483	41970	45707	42161	46815	50719
24972	29459	33196	37483	41970	45707	42161	46815	50719	55173

Cashflow Two: the first year

		January	February	March	April	May
Income						
Lettings	£77,000	4000	4000	4000	5000	6000
TOTAL income	£77,000	4000	4000	4000	5000	6000
Expenditure						
Administrator	£ 15,000	1250	1250	1250	1250	1250
Cleaner	£ 6,996	583	583	583	583	583
Caretaker	£ 6,996	583	583	583	583	583
Heat	£ 2,000			500		
Light	£ 1,000			250		
Office costs	£ 3,000	3000				
Phone	£ 750	150			200	
Stationery	£ 1,007	600	37	37	37	37
Maintenance	£ 1,500	1000				500
Minor repairs	£ 504	42	42	42	42	42
Rent	£ 15,000	1250	1250	1250	1250	1250
Publicity	£ 1,995	1500	45	45	45	45
Cleaning materials	£ 996	83	83	83	83	83
Major repairs fund	£ 15,000	1250	1250	1250	1250	1250
Supplies	£ 504	42	42	42	42	42
Insurance	£ 7,000	7000				
Equipment	£ 9,991	8000	181	181	181	181
TOTAL expenditure	£89,239	26333	5346	6096	5546	5846
Opening balance		0	−22333	−23679	−25775	−26321
Closing balance		−22333	−23679	−25775	−26321	−26167

Note: Inflation is not included

Cycle Two: Design and Plan

	June	July	August	September	October	November	December
	6000	6000	4000	8000	10000	10000	10000
	6000	6000	4000	8000	10000	10000	10000
	1250	1250	1250	1250	1250	1250	1250
	583	583	583	583	583	583	583
	583	583	583	583	583	583	583
	500			500			500
	250			250			250
		200			200		
	37	37	37	37	37	37	37
	42	42	42	42	42	42	42
	1250	1250	1250	1250	1250	1250	1250
	45	45	45	45	45	45	45
	83	83	83	83	83	83	83
	1250	1250	1250	1250	1250	1250	1250
	42	42	42	42	42	42	42
	181	181	181	181	181	181	181
	6096	5546	5346	6096	5546	5346	6096
	−26167	−26263	−25809	−27155	−25251	−20797	−16143
	−26263	−25809	−27155	−25251	−20797	−16143	−12239

Sensitivity of the income stream

The first year's budget in the figure on pages 162–3 shows a gradually rising income month on month. A thorough analysis should be made of this kind of figure. The first month's income is based on lettings that the team are absolutely sure will be there on the first week. These must already be booked before they are entered on the budget.

Next identify the grounds for assuming this level of increase over the first year. There may be enquiries already received or levels of bookings promised that make it possible for the building to be fully booked this way. Justify it to yourselves – thoroughly. In fact, if this positive scenario were to be achieved, financial stability would soon be well established.

On the whole, people who are prepared to try new things are optimistic people. There is a third and more realistic way to explore the cashflow. The sum of the annual costs on budget (pages 160–1) is £82,293. If the project attracted lettings at 70 per cent of the level given in the schedule of use, the project would still be viable. Below that figure it is not going to pay its way. The team can conclude that the project running at between 70 and 100 per cent of the probable use would remain viable. In monitoring progress this can be a standard to watch for by looking at lettings, not only at cash in the bank. If the level of bookings slips below 70 per cent a staff cut or an increase in hourly letting rates may be necessary.

Another sensitivity will be that some months will have more bookings than others. August may be low for regular groups but the summer may have more wedding reception bookings. As far as possible use real figures and real experience to make these judgements while planning. Other hall facilities in similar areas to your church's will have records that indicate the pattern of bookings, and they may be happy to share their experience.

Capital budgets and cashflow

When preparing for building work similar budgets of expenditure can be made by the quantity surveyor for the projected expenditure on fees and builders for the duration of the works.

Most realistically, all money for capital works should be in the bank before work starts. At times churches have planned to continue to fundraise as the project goes along and have come unstuck. For example, a church planned to sell some land, but when the sale fell through had to maintain a very expensive bridging loan for several years. Money already formally offered from outside agencies may suffer occasional significant slips – I heard of a promised regeneration grant that was withdrawn when the geographical area of the church was reclassified as outside the regeneration zone.

If your project is planning to reclaim money from the Listed Places of Worship Grant Scheme (the VAT counterbalancing scheme), ensure that the time delay between when VAT is paid out by the church and the repayment by the scheme does not present a problem deficit on the projection of payments.

Responsible financial management systems

Plan to set up a handbook of financial management, including required practice in dealing with the income for bookings (should it be cheques or will cash do?). How can cash be safeguarded? How can fraud be prevented? All orders for items should be within budget and only made by agreed persons. How will book-keeping be done and who will do it? How will deposits be returned? Cheques would be advisable, only made payable to the person who made the first payment, not someone else. There will be many more items to add; most dioceses now make recommendations to church treasurers on what these measures should be. For further help try *A Practical Guide to Financial Management for Charities and Voluntary Organizations* by Kate Sayer, published by the Directory of Social Change, 1998.

Summary

The financial viability of the regenerated church has to be planned before any major plan is enacted. Ensure that the project that is being set up will not take the church further into difficulty. Using cashflow projections is a key tool in understanding the future viability of the church's activity.

The business plan

The business plan is the document that enables an organization or a business to ensure that all the threads of their activity, their planned targets and the resources to meet those targets are planned in the best possible way for success. Success is not necessarily an issue of profit, but can be the benefits delivered or the values fulfilled or ongoing activity made sustainable. The business plan will show that the organization will deliver these targets in the most effective way, that is ensuring the highest level of benefit to recipients. It will show that this is efficient, that the resources are used well and carefully and that time, money and skills are not being wasted while producing the target. It will also show that the delivery of targets is done in a way that is in harmony with the organization's values. For churches who may have set out on this journey without exploring and writing their own Plan for Mission, it will be more difficult to assess that the preferred way forward is in keeping with the church's values.

Within the voluntary sector as a whole, not just among churches, there is a basic contents list for a business plan. If the document will only be used internally this is less significant, but if the church will be using the document to make a case to potential funders, such elements should be included. Then there is a wide variation of content when it comes to the form of *delivery of activities* that will achieve the church's targets. I am including elements for a multi-faceted project, but for many churches only some of those headings are needed. Fundamentally *delivery* includes any description of resources management essential to achieve the regeneration targets. For example, the business plan may describe a project that includes no building construction work, so the *building* section may be dropped; but the *management of facilities* may still be needed.

Ensure that the business plan robustly reinforces viability and identifies clearly the outside contributions that will be necessary for viability:

- Construction costs (after feasibility work by architect)
- Capital funding
- Revenue projections
- Realistic revenue income streams
- Optimal revenue costs

Much of the material that will be incorporated in the business plan consists of the working documents prepared in earlier stages of the Development Cycle.

The business plan ought to be no longer than 25 pages, but supporting information should be appended.

Executive summary

The business plan starts with an executive summary. This is one page that summarizes the direction taken, why it is being taken and the resources that will be expended to achieve the project. It is best written after the rest of the business plan is drawn together.

Background information

The organization

Include information on the church: its legal status,[28] its location, its management structure, staff, existing programmes and activities, building and land assets (as relevant) and membership.

---

28 Churches are excepted charities, that is they are registered with the Charity Commission but do not have registration numbers. Where a charity number is required it is often acceptable for a church to use the Inland Revenue registration number that is used for claiming Gift Aid.

Include information on the people developing the project, the church council, their skills and experiences (and, for building projects, the design and management professionals). Outside people can then be reassured that the organization is able to deliver the project.

SWOT analysis

Update and summarize the SWOT analysis worked on earlier in the Development Cycle, thinking carefully about presentation as the document may be read by people who have not been involved in the development process. A diagram that fits a single page is ideal; more detail and explanation can be appended. This presentation of the document will include the opportunities that came out of meeting local council officers and others, from among whom the team has identified part-nerships in the regeneration of the church.

Option appraisal

Update and summarize the Option Appraisal drawn up when possibilities were being considered. A summary can be presented, for example, as a one-page version of the diagram on page 86, with summary notes.

Local needs and demands

The Option Appraisal and the visits to local people will have uncovered the statistics about the needs locally as well as direct contact with people who are asking for the facilities or services.

The demographic information can be included in graphs. It is worth carefully selecting from the available information and creating a few specific graphs, not simply importing them, for example, from the borough's website.

Include a summary of information collected from initial visits to local organizations, residents, council departments and others. This will have resulted in opportunities the team took up, so it should reinforce the chosen Strategy and help develop partnerships.

The building issues

Regeneration in most churches will include review and realistic assessment of their buildings: underuse, state of repair, lack of facilities and management issues. Resultant solutions in the light of the strategy are included in the delivery section below.

The strategy

State briefly the way the church is going forward.

Ongoing activities

Include a summary of the ongoing programme of the regenerated church after the changes are made. A good summary may be a sample weekly schedule identifying groups and programmes that will happen regularly. It could equally be a calendar of events or some other clear indication of how much will happen, for whom and how often.

Outcomes

Summarize the outcomes identified on page 121. Ensure that necessary explanation is added for people who may not have been party to the development process.

Outputs

Summarize the outputs identified on page 121.

Required inputs

Summarize all the resources, staff and money, building repair and alteration that will be necessary to achieve both the outcomes and outputs. Do not focus on building work only: if the delivery of positive benefits requires the establishment of programmes of activity after the building is complete, these should be included. New staff requirements should be listed. Include the sum to be raised for capital works and the revenue cost and how this will be met.

Risk analysis

Include a well-summarized risk analysis for the regeneration project. Again, additional material or explanations may be appended. But include enough material here to ensure that the reader can see that the strategy has been thoroughly assessed and the major risks have been identified and action prepared or taken. Many of the major risks will be addressed in the next section, that is the description of how the regeneration project will be delivered. For example, management elements will include how health and safety will be ensured or what new staff are required.

Delivery of the project

The building

Include the written brief which the team gave to the architect with any updates that were subsequently made. The full version can be appended.

Include an account of the construction works summarized in words, and it is useful to append a straightforward plan of the building identifying changes that are planned. This should be accompanied by a quantity surveyor's budget – including the cost of fees and VAT.

Include a breakdown of ongoing running and repair costs (this will back up the figures used in financial projections that are to be accrued in a Sinking Fund for future building works).

Cleaning and caretaking should be addressed, as a busy attractive building will only stay attractive if well cared-for.

Any outside funder interested in viability and sustainability will want to ensure that their investment is well used in a building well cared-for.

Management of facilities

Extended use will always involve more staff time. List the staff who will be employed to care for the facilities and, where this involves a new job being created, append the job description. Expect to include at least a cleaner and a caretaker, whose job will include out-of-hours keyholding, and a facilities manager. The latter may seem a big step to take; however, if new policies are required, lots of new users of the building expected and a wide range of new use needs to be established, the work will be more than a vicar can take up in their spare time, even if they have the skills. Each of these jobs may be part-time and will have been built into the budget to ensure that increased use of the building can pay for their work. For smaller projects some churches depend on volunteers for management, in which case just volunteer expenses need to be included, but job descriptions are still helpful.

Policies
A well-used community building should expect to have policies in place for health and safety, equal opportunities, access, marketing, letting policy and booking systems, a financial handbook controlling how money is handled, and policies for staff management and appraisal. These and other necessary policies should be in written form available to staff and to others who wish to enquire about them. They may be prepared by staff rather than the committee but are essential in risk management. Summarize them in the business plan and do not append them if they are large documents.[29]

---

29 Sample policies for some of these items are available in *Making Church Buildings Work* (see n. 19).

Staff for community projects

Where the extension of facilities in the regenerated church includes the church setting up its own community projects, welfare, arts or education, several additional elements should be included.

Criteria for the staff
Community activity requires appropriately qualified professional staff. Being a Christian as well as being qualified may be attractive to the church but may be unnecessary for the job, so ensure that job descriptions (appended to the Business Plan) do not take the church outside what is permitted by Equal Opportunities legislation.[30]

If a project will run for more than the occasional session it should perhaps have its own management committee with the skills to ensure that professional standards are maintained in all aspects of its work. Such names can be included in the business plan. This can still be a sub-committee of the church council with its own terms of reference (appended if the project will be a new venture).

The community project budget
Do include the community project budget so that its viability and sustainability is evident to readers of the business plan. In the intense process of sorting out capital works on the building it is easy to overlook the development of the budget for ongoing community work. This element is especially crucial if the community project will be grant dependent; a fundraising plan that stands up to scrutiny will be required.

Partnerships

Many church regeneration projects are made effective and far-reaching through partnership with other agencies in the

---

30 More details and explanation are available in *Making Church Buildings Work* (see n. 19).

neighbourhood. The research and development processes of the two cycles of development covered to date will have identified such partners. Some will continue as friends in a network of mutual support and common interest. Some will progress to being partners in construction and delivery of services. Various boroughs have created such partnerships with churches.

The business plan should identify partners and how the partnership will work. Joint activity should be described and the limitations of the partnership defined. Such elements will have come from the dialogue with partners and will be subject to careful perusal of the legal ramifications so that both partners are protected in the case of things going wrong. The legal status of the partnership should be stated. The details in the business plan should be sufficient for the reader to ensure that the legal issues are being properly addressed as well as the activities.

Finance

The work undertaken on finance (see pages 151–66) should be summarized and the figures appended, that is the revenue budget and cashflow projections.

A summary of the financial management procedures should be included if new procedures are being added because of the extension of activity.

Marketing

Outside agencies, in reading the business plan, may want to be sure that any extension of facilities to which they are contributing is really being extended to everyone who lives in the neighbourhood. The church may not be known to everyone, and its new activities will almost certainly not be known unless good work has been undertaken consulting with and informing local people of progress.

If a new or refurbished community hall or meeting rooms

are being created, then a simple programme should be in place to let all those who might wish to use the facilities know that they are opening. This may be as simple as an advertisement in the local paper, a news release, leafleting and posters. In villages the church newsletter often goes to every home, and this could be adequate.

For community projects offering a programme of activity, for children or other target groups, you can include a summary of how you will ensure that all those within the catchment will know about the service. It will not be adequate to do this by word-of-mouth, as this can result in only an 'in-group' benefiting.

Fundraising

Since most church regeneration projects are undertaken because the church needs new life breathing into it or to push out beyond its present boundaries, most will need to raise funds from outside sources to make the new project happen.

A strategy can be included in the business plan, showing the methods and targets of the fundraising programme. Include internal fundraising (in the church), as well as fundraising in the local neighbourhood among people who will benefit from the regeneration of the church, with local council and regeneration agencies and from outside trusts and the National Lottery.

Critical path

On my very first church regeneration project a very helpful business partner showed how to put all the issues and agendas and schedules into a critical path. It was one of the most useful lessons I learned on that project.

The summary critical path that is included in the business plan will indicate to the team, the church and outside people that work is going forward in a systematic way that will facilitate the achievement of the aims of the church as expressed in the business plan.

The figure on pages 176–7 is a simple version that illustrates the key principle, which is to identify which tasks have to be completed before others can begin. The result is a programme of activity clearly identifying which tasks should be tackled now and which ones have to wait till later.

The details of each church's projects will of course be different from this over-simplified example. Laying out a chart like this enables you to see, for example, the need to set out the community project even while planning for building work is still under way. If the community project is going to begin as soon as the building opens then fundraising should start even while the fundraising for the building is under way. Equally, whenever the start of the community activity is set it is clear that 15 to 18 months' activity will need to precede that opening.

Note also that there are activities that have to be completed before others can take place at all. Building construction cannot start until fundraising is complete, and if that is delayed – and the bigger the sum the more likely this is – then all *dependent* activity is delayed.

It is normally a mistake to use such a critical path as a defined timeline except in a very few circumstances. Use the months as indicative not absolute. Use it as a guide to inform you of the impact of change in one element on all other aspects of the strategy. If the fundraising for construction slips by several months you can see that the appointment of the worker to the community project is delayed.

There are many more elements on the detailed critical path of most churches engaging in a regeneration project. Brainstorm these together in the team before one or two people draft the critical path. Then ask the church council to contribute as well, so as many interrelated issues as possible can be identified.

Once the critical path has been drawn up (it's worth drawing it on Excel or a similar program, as changes in the detail as you progress can then be used to produce a revised critical path) the team can easily prioritize its work and *see* that not everything has to or even can happen at once.

Critical Path

	Jan	Feb	Mar	Apr	May	Jun	Jul	Aug
Finish building scheme design	▓	▓						
Apply for faculty and listed building consent			▓	▓	▓			
Fundraise for capital				▓	▓	▓	▓	▓
Complete design and tender								
Begin construction								
Opening of building								
Agree partnership activity	▓	▓	▓					
Fundraise for community project				▓	▓	▓	▓	▓
Agree legal aspects of partnership	▓	▓	▓					
Engage lawyer to create documents				▓	▓	▓	▓	▓
Recruit staff								
Set up and promote activities								
Commence community activity								
Other aspects of strategy								

Cycle Two: Design and Plan

Sep	Oct	Nov	Dec	Jan	Feb	Mar	Apr	May	Jun	Jul
▓										
	▓	▓	▓							
				▓	▓	▓	▓	▓	▓	
										▓
▓										
▓	▓	▓	▓							
				▓	▓	▓	▓			
								▓	▓	
										▓

Summary

The completed business plan is always in draft form; just as the critical path is adapted, so the business plan will also change over time. It does however give a clear overview to anyone reading it, both the big picture and the detail of how it will be delivered.

Expect to review the church business plan every year, just to ensure that you have not stepped outside your intended targets and that annual targets are appropriate and relevant to the big picture. After three years most organizations find they need to rewrite substantially.

Report

The business plan should be presented to the church council (in full) and to the church members (in summary). The financial commitments that are involved in enacting the plan are significant, and those to whom the church belongs must within reason be confident that the plan is well designed and planned and that it will be viable and sustainable in the medium to long term.

9

Cycle Three:
Activating the Plan

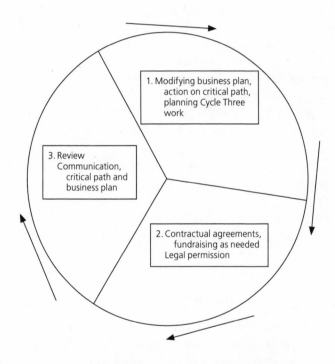

1. Modifying business plan, action on critical path, planning Cycle Three work

2. Contractual agreements, fundraising as needed Legal permission

3. Review Communication, critical path and business plan

Cycle Three takes the Strategy and planning and turns it into reality. A strong and potentially viable and sustainable church regeneration project becomes active. Actions will now be taken that cost money in addition to the time and effort of clergy and volunteers.

Review the business plan and set up an action plan for the team

Review the critical path and identify the set of actions that are needed to make everything happen. Write out a team action plan, highlighting the first tasks to be undertaken by whom, by when and at what cost.

By reviewing the SWOT analysis that came at the beginning of the development process the team may find that skills offered by some members can come into play here. People with a professional background may volunteer help to ensure that the detailed brief over building or legal advice, or about community or council partnerships, can be thoroughly explored and prepared. It is not advisable to employ church members in professional roles as this can cause too many problems later. For example, the architect in the congregation may not be a specialist in the kind of work the church needs or may insist on a process that is too expensive. Once mistakes are made or problems arise, fellowship may be broken and that is too high a cost.

The kinds of professional work that advisers will now be asked for will cost considerable sums of money. Agree with each professional what their work will cost as a sum or a rate. If you accept a rate – say £85 per hour – then ask for an estimate of how many hours the work may take so the church can be prepared for the bills.

Scheme design by the architect

Setting out on the detailed design is a new stage for making payment to the architect and may be calculated as a percentage of the estimated cost of the building works. The architect is entitled to staged payments, so some money will be due now in addition to the hourly rate or lump sum the church paid for the feasibility stage. For fundraising purposes a plan of the new work and a quantity surveyor's budget will be adequate for making applications to outside funders and need not involve further significant expense. However, the applications to outside bodies for permission to go ahead do require much more work.

Dialogue with the architect should by now have reached a point of an acceptable design, at least to the church. If, as recommended, the team has informally consulted the Diocesan Advisory Committee and local Conservation Officers you may have a fairly clear idea whether these essential authorities are generally in favour of the church plan.

The architect will now prepare for applying for faculty, for planning permission and for listed building consent as appropriate.

Some schemes for new building works or alterations may get permission rather readily, but others, especially in or near to a listed church, may take a lot longer. At times the authorities can and will ask for a complete rethink. It is for this reason that an early preliminary approach is recommended, as the architect can then take into account the responses of the authorities in the way the design progresses, and the permission process may be smoother. It will also save money as incomplete plans cost less to change than a complete set.

Legal permission

Certain kinds of change of use need planning permission. Other kinds of change of use need permission from the church authorities through the faculty process.

Church buildings are zoned, from the planning permission point of view, in a category that includes both GP surgeries and pre-school nurseries. Community activities in the church may be considered church activity and not a change of use. However, many other activities would need permission as they are outside permitted use. For example, a church café would need planning permission as change of use, and permission would be needed to put up the café sign board outside the church. Any trading activity will require permission.

Churches, not church halls, as consecrated spaces are subject to separate laws. At present only a licence may be granted to a tenant, not a lease, in order to protect the status of the building. Potential tenants are naturally unsure about licences as they give far less security to the tenant and more to the church. If and when the law changes it may be possible to lease out a minority space within a church; seek specialist legal advice as the present plan for the church to lease space may in fact result in a lack of resources for mission in future years.

Repairing the church hall for continuing use will require Building Regulations Compliance, which is fundamentally a method of the local authority ensuring that appropriate standards are maintained in the way that the building work is done and the safety of the resultant space.[31]

The architect, the Diocesan Advisory Committee secretary and the archdeacon are key advisers in the permission processes the church will need to follow.

Allow plenty of time to process all the legal aspects of the regeneration project; this can run in parallel with the fundraising process.

Sale of property

The church may hold property – land or buildings – that it wishes to sell to finance regeneration.

Some property may belong to the church or church council, other property will belong to the diocese and still more to a combination of the church and Church Commissioners.

The church

If a church building's use is going to change significantly, then the church may be made redundant; that is, it is deconsecrated. All or part may be later re-consecrated as a licensed worship space.

---

31 See Maggie Durran, *Making Church Buildings Work*, Canterbury Press, 2005.

The redundant church is in the ownership of the diocese. So making a church redundant with a view to sale and use of the funds for the regeneration (maybe with new worship space) can only be done with the co-operation and agreement of the diocese. When a church is sold some money also returns to the Church Commissioners, and the balance belongs to the diocese because of the redundant church status.

The hall and clergy housing

The church council may collectively 'own' the church hall or clergy housing but because of the nature of their trusteeship they will need diocesan permission to sell the hall and put the money into something else. Do note that if the church council sells a hall to invest the money in the church, it does not change the status of the ownership of the church; the investment cannot be taken out later even if the church is sold. A legal agreement may be made with the diocese before the change happens, so consult the diocesan staff.

The vicarage

The vicarage is owned by the diocese and it is maintained and repaired by them.

All this means that a complicated transaction to release capital for regeneration, from the combination of church assets, requires the assent of lots of people, including: archdeacon, Diocesan Advisory Committee, diocesan board of finance and property department, Redundant Churches Uses Committee and the Church Commissioners. Despite the complexity, many churches do land deals that release capital to benefit both church and diocese. For example, the diocese may buy a piece of land from the church for a new vicarage (giving money to the church) and subsequently sell off the old vicarage. But the sale of the vicarage on its own would not provide any money for the church!

Fundraising from church and outside sources

Contacts made during the external exploration for possibilities and for developing partnerships, in Cycles One and Two of the development cycle, are very likely to produce funding partners as well as project partners. The task may now be a matter of preparing all the necessary written material to bring forward that finance.

Similarly, a church that has worked through the steps of the development cycle including the preparation of the business plan has the raw material on which a number of different fundraising activities can be based.

Since fundraising contains a great deal of detail, this section is designed to give an overview, and if more direction is needed then *The UK Church Fundraising Handbook* gives guidelines on all sorts of fundraising.

For each of the following sources of funding there are different approaches, often using different skills. Creating a wider fundraising team, bringing in those skills, may be a wise move at this stage.

Before you start, it is vital that a *THANK YOU system* is set up. This is a detailed administrative task that ensures that every donor receives a personal thank you letter and each is invited to consultative or celebratory events. I hear regularly from donors to churches that they made a gift or grant and no one even acknowledged it! Every donor is identifying their allegiance and commitment to the church – this person is a friend! They will be friends for life if the church takes simple steps to build the relationship.

Church members

As the most committed, most involved people and 'owners' of the project church, members are the most likely and comparatively the most generous donors. Various approaches have been made to attract donations from members. Some churches have simply announced the fundraising drive and left members to decide. Others hold a presentation evening with a request for donations. One church, after receiving generous donations (£55,000) from parishioners after a letter and open evenings, sent a similar letter to each person on the church electoral roll and received £60,000. Some churches have had individual meetings with all church members to explain and answer questions and then invited donations. Churches with a tradition of Gift Days have made building projects the subject and received tremendous gifts. The skills needed are interpersonal from people respected by members. Clergy have to be careful not to ask emotionally vulnerable people for money, as this can create pastoral problems. Prepare a small package of information for each member, choose the communication method that suits your congregation and invite generosity.

Remember too that members are likely to leave a legacy to the church if advised that this will be helpful, so include a legacy leaflet in the package.

Local groups and residents

Local residents may respond positively to a personally addressed letter with an attractive brochure enclosed,[32] giving details of the project, the benefits that they can expect from it, information on how to give and postal information. Many communities find that local people have a loyalty to their church that has not been expressed in church attendance. Hold a presentation evening for those who want more information before giving.

Writing skills are needed for the brochure and accompanying letter. Each letter must be personally addressed[33] (never to 'the occupier') and individually signed by the vicar. A small work party can do everything except the signing.

Local groups will respond to partnership and activity

---

32 For more guidance see Maggie Durran, *The UK Church Fundraising Handbook*, Canterbury Press, 2003.
33 Try www.192.com for information on who lives in your parish or neighbourhood.

together. As you plan local fundraising events, invite other local charities to join you. See this as building friendships and partnerships, as well as raising money.

Trusts

There are large numbers of trusts that will help with everything from church repairs to fitting new facilities. They will also fund revenue for community projects.

Skills needed are writing and verbal, not so much passion as concise, clear, informative and attractive descriptions. Some donors will need business plan information; all will need budget summaries and financial information. Clear information on the benefits that will result for local people are fundamental to outside funders.

Sources of information on trusts are given in *The UK Church Fundraising Handbook*.

Local authority

Apart from small streams such as Community Chest, most of the relevant streams of funding from this source would have become apparent during the exploration and partnership stages of work. If they did not, those who met council officers and councillors can now, with good planning in hand, phone their contacts and ask advice about funding sources. Particularly if there are council partnerships in the development, this is likely to be a rich source of funds. The application procedures will be lengthy, as all such financing is subject to government audit. Skills needed include the ability to translate from church-speak to local authority-speak! It is worth finding a volunteer or someone through the local Council for the Voluntary Sector to help.

Regeneration

Exploring potential regeneration partnerships will probably have brought all the potential funding connections to the fore. Expect tediously long and strangely intricate forms to be completed. Each one is different. Be sure to accurately and appropriately answer every question. It is likely that for some questions you will not be able to understand how this fits the church context; officers are normally extremely helpful.

Lottery

Each of the Lottery boards has long application packs. The larger the amount asked for, the longer the process and the greater the quantity of paperwork. Each also has very particular angles on how it distributes funding. Expect to use the regeneration project business plan with some parts re-angled to suit the information required by the Lottery distributor. Each has a website giving information on the funding streams. Thankfully, there are at present moves to use introductory application forms followed by more complex forms and information production for projects that fit the requirements. It is becoming normal for the Lottery distributor to provide a casework officer who may, in the case of the Big Lottery, help the applicant with the form-filling.

While a group may suggest bullet points for answering the questions, one person will need to sit down for several days of uninterrupted time to fill out the forms. Like regeneration bodies, the Lottery distributors have to stand up to significant levels of auditing, so the process is almost tediously complex. Stick with it.

Major donors

All kinds of charities get major donations from rich individuals. Unfortunately most churches do not have rich individuals living in the parish. Those that do may make special approaches to people they know, inviting their donations or inviting them to become patrons and to encourage others to give. Interpersonal skills are needed.

If your church has a catchment of the rich and famous, like

a few city centre churches and cathedrals, and you want to raise a very large amount, some millions of pounds, it may be worth contacting a fundraising company that specializes in big gift fundraising, as they have experience in locating and asking the right donors.

Companies

It may be that major companies are best approached like major individual donors, but for most parish churches it is worth making an appointment with the managing directors of local businesses large and small and asking how they might help you. Do expect various contributions in kind and not much in donations. However, some of my best fundraising breakthroughs have happened when business partners put their name down as supporters.

Previous donors

Ask someone with administrative skills to go through the old records of the church to find out who has previously given to the church. This will be individuals, trusts and others who have expressed some level of interest and commitment in the past. Provided someone said a proper thank you and showed appreciation for the donation, the same people may be interested in giving again. In terms of contacts it is always easier to move from warm to hot than from cold to hot.

Summary

Identify the kinds of fundraising that are suited to your project.

Identify the people with the skills needed to make the best applications.

Follow up all donations with a *thank you* and invitations to future events.

Keep records of all donors, who, if the church maintains the relationship, may be donors again the next time you need money.

Remember to ask all individuals, members and non-members, to consider leaving a legacy to the church.

Formal agreements on partnerships

The legal agreements that undergird all partnerships, from the joint management of a welfare project to a lease on a community space, operate on legal principles that should be understood before signing. Legal agreements are prepared by the lawyers with a view to protecting the interests of their client. So they are couched in terms about things going wrong, not about good working relationships when things are going well. The more significant the partnership, in money or facilities or joint work, the more complex the legal agreement. Lawyers from both parties will end up meeting and arguing what seem ludicrous points but that are essential over time.

To prepare well for the stage when lawyers get involved, meet the new partner and talk about the kind of relationship that the church is planning. Look back for some of the issues the church may wish to safeguard and add those that also define a good relationship: how you will work together, how you will resolve disagreements, what joint activity you will undertake. Where joint management is concerned, ensure fair representation on committees; and where it is in the best interests of the church it may wish to have a right of veto (hopefully never used, but it may serve to protect the church in the future). On the whole churches have proved to be far too keen to give away rights and create agreements to their own disadvantage.

Most importantly, never make an agreement that alienates an asset unnecessarily. Many tenancies on church halls give away all the church's rights, from right of access to ability to take the hall back in the future. The lease takes the property outside the Landlord and Tenant Act, which would allow for say five-yearly reviews, at which time the landlord could take back the building for their own use, in order to raise higher levels of rent. Presumably the hall is not needed at the time, but so often after a few years, with a new vicar and new mission activity, the church needs the hall but cannot get it back for another twenty years. Ensure that agreements are in the best interests of the church of the future, not just the one of today, and taking less income might be better than alienating the space.

For a commercial lease or one with a statutory authority the best option is probably to ask diocesan lawyers and commercial surveyors to work out the best deal they can for the church. The commercial clients will be operating on that basis and the kindliness of the church people will work to the church's disadvantage if you are not extremely careful to take the right advice.

Above all, allow plenty of time for the professionals to look at and prepare legal agreements. Never under any circumstances allow a tenant to move in before the lawyer says the church can allow them in; the consequence would be that the prospective tenant, without a formal agreement, achieves rights under the law that the church would never wish for. For any ongoing tenancy or regular significant letting an early conversation with the diocesan surveyors or property department is advisable.

Summary

Allow plenty of time.

Do not alienate building assets from the church of the future.

Get ecclesiastical legal advice as early as possible.

Let the lawyer defend the church's interests in the negotiations.

Prepare construction programme and disruption plans

The professional team working on the church's building plans will prepare a construction programme. Some issues may be so obvious to the design team that they don't think to raise it early on: such as that the church's own programme of activity will have to be moved out of the building in order for work to happen. Sometimes work may be going on in part of the building and use may continue, say, in the chancel, but that is not always possible; or if it is possible it may be considerably more expensive. The construction project manager will have to take into account access and health and safety in looking at this question, and if special constraints have to be imposed on the builder, what costs will be incurred. For example, if all building materials and tools have to be stored every weekend so the church people can use the space, part of every Friday afternoon and Monday morning will be used in the clearing and setting up processes, all at the client's expense. A total of a half day lost each week will add as much as 10 per cent to the cost of the project. Start talking early on with the project manager.

My own church, with a major one-year building programme that will require us to completely evacuate the building, has set up a forward planning committee that is looking at moving furniture and moveable items to storage, planning church activity while we are out of the building, the move back into the building and anything else to do with disruption.

Building is a dusty and invasive activity. Fittings of the church, from furniture to wall plaques, may be protected by the builder at the beginning of the building contract. All other movable or precious items should be addressed by the church. What would the project manager recommend? Get professional advice on what to do with the organ or the piano.

Consider the people during the programme. Most long-standing members will have habits that are part of the creative familiarity of the church, so consider these carefully, everything from service sheets and hymn books to candles and prayer requests. If the building is evacuated, how will drop-in churchgoers find their way to worship services, or even present members when the change is first made? How will special events or festival services that local people are familiar with be organized and communication set up?

It can be emotionally difficult at first to return to an altered church building and feel at home. It is worth creating special liturgy for leaving the church, taking symbolic items in procession from the church, not only the liturgical ones but those that represent familiarity and adminstration. Consider hassocks, toys from the crêche, collection plates, palm branches from Palm Sunday, choir robes and so on. Then just as they were processed out, create a new procession and homecoming for the first service after the construction phase, owning and embodying in liturgy the feelings of the congregation in the context of change as well as the thanksgiving for the work achieved.

Prepare people, especially those for whom change is difficult, for the changes that will result when community groups are using the church on a daily basis. Many things will not be as flexible as they were, from times to arrange flowers to access to pray or clean. Preparation will mitigate confusion and conflict.

Summary

A few hours preparation will save a multitude of confusions. A smaller version of the critical path can be used to identify everyone and all kinds of work that will be disrupted and plans made to minimize the impact.

Major presentation to all stakeholders

Everyone with an interest in the church's regeneration programme, from donors to potential beneficiaries, is a stakeholder. There are several key elements of a regeneration programme that can make or break these relationships. The disruption considerations above are mostly about church members, but do consider more widely.

Everyone who has donated anything to the regeneration should receive a good thank-you. Letters should go promptly to everyone who has donated cash or another significant gift.

Along with this there should be an administrative task that ensures that these donors are updated as the programme proceeds and are invited to all celebratory events. Not everyone, for example council officers, will come to a church service, but they might come to a lunchtime reception with a short speech, drinks and a buffet. For major regeneration work the church may therefore plan more than one celebratory event, targeting different people.

Major funders such as the English Heritage and the Heritage Lottery Fund seldom receive adequate thanks, despite the size of their contribution. Thanks are in order. The Heritage Lottery Fund does supply a plaque that acknowledges their contribution for display in the church, but a church could prepare its own permanent display acknowledging various donors to the project.

When the regeneration project involves capital works followed by an ongoing programme of community activity it is good to keep all the stakeholders up to date with ongoing success. A newsletter with a mailing list of all those involved in any way in the regeneration would be one straightforward method, set up before the church regeneration team disbands from its task.

Review revenue projections with church council

As adjustments have been made to the plans for the regeneration of the church through the cycles of development, the revenue projections for the ongoing church and/or community facilities will have changed. It is crucially important that the original financial values, setting up financial sustainability, are maintained. To ensure the projections remain viable a good process is to update the cashflow spreadsheet on a regular basis, checking the impact of changes before agreeing to them. A change of potential tenant, a reduction in space or opportunity or a delay in a tenant moving in, may all impact on the plan and challenge the workability of the budget. When set up, the budget may have held some contingency, and that will provide a buffer; but it is better not to get to the brink of viability, rather to make early plans to mitigate problems as they arise.

Set up a management or steering committee for the ongoing project

Often the people who have the skills and the drive for running a project are not those who made the regeneration project happen in the first place. The processes of managing an on-going project, whether running hall centre facilities or a welfare project for the disadvantaged, are related but different. So expect at some point to set up a management committee for the ongoing regenerated church and disband the team that have worked on it in the Development Cycle. Clearly there will have to be an overlap as the regeneration working team have a detailed knowledge of how the business plan works and this should be carried forward. But, for example, if the welfare project will work with children, there may be potential committee members who are childcare professionals and who would be an asset to the committee, even though they would have shied away from the development team.[34]

Consider the variety of skills the church will need for ongoing management and, while the construction phase is still running, set up the new committee and begin the processes of appointing staff. At the completion of building work the church can celebrate together the end of the building works (which are only the means to delivering new benefits) and the beginning of the work which will continue a programme of beneficial activity for church and neighbourhood.

---

34 *Making Church Buildings Work* (see n. 31) contains much information on managing and maintaining community and church projects.

Appendix

Assessing Sustainability

The questions raised in this section are based on the Sustainability matrix[35] in the book *Building Sustainability in the Balance*.[36] It is possible and straightforward to achieve a numeric assessment of whether a church building can be made sustainable. Using a matrix of uniform questions with numeric answers also facilitates a study of a number of churches and comparison between them, so conclusions about their comparative ability to become sustainable are made on a level playing field. The method allows us to assess all buildings against the same set of criteria, so in the case of churches it aids us in identifying those we believe must be saved and makes evident the key reasons for this.

The social and cultural issues (and here that includes the religious issues) that are significant to every church building are assessed alongside the more physical characteristics.

The questions raised in *Building Sustainability in the Balance* have here been changed into church language but fundamentally relate to the same issues.

Location: Has it got economic, social, commercial, aesthetic value in this location? What potential is there?

Economic. Can it become financially self-sustaining?
Commercial. Can added uses increase income, leading to sustainability?

---

35 For more information contact King Sturge, 7 Stratford Place, London WIC IST.
36 Sarah Sayce, Anthony Walker and Angus Macintosh, *Building Sustainability in the Balance*, E G Books, 2004.

Social. Has it or might it have a key function in the local social fabric? Measures the degree to which buildings and users contribute to the local environment.

Aesthetic. What is its importance to the local streetscape and sense of quality of life, bearing in mind that an empty unused building soon loses perceived value?

Is the building efficient?

Is it used every day for a number of people appropriate to its size, standing – is it fit for purpose?

Is the cost of running the building readily met from its income? If the market value of the building/site were deposited in a high-interest deposit account would the interest be more than the building is producing in income and value of use?

Is it efficient land use, or could the whole site be better used?

What is the tenure; can the building be changed without loss because of covenants etc.?

Is transport access good for current use and potential new use?

Is the fabric in good repair and can it readily be kept in good repair?

Is it suitable to present use, and does it have potential for added use every day?

Social questions

Is the church attractive to and valued by people other than church members, attracting them to bring additional functions here?

Is it important to members, the church at large, local residents and wider audiences? Is it listed, and what grade and for what reasons? If it is important to and valued by local people, organizations and agencies, they should help pay for it.

Is it liked – passionately – by members and wider users and audiences?

Is it disabled-accessible, complying with health and safety criteria, warm enough, light enough, or can it readily be made so?

As a working environment, is it fit for purpose for staff and for volunteers, safe and welcoming? Are staff facilities appropriately fitted? If more uses were added, could it be made into a good working environment?

Environmental issues

Is it productive, that is are users satisfied with it as a space?

Is it inflexible?

Does it lack natural light?

Does it create undesirable emissions?

Energy. With concern for the depletion of natural resources and carbon emissions, does it have a suitable heating system (with new-style boiler)? Is there unnecessary heat loss or air leakage?

Internally the issue may be cost, while externally the concern will be global warming.

Embodied energy. Energy and resources (other than money) were expended to make this building. Replacing it would cost an even greater use of energy and resources (regardless of money), so can the life of this building be extended to optimize the energy investment value? That is, in terms of the investment of resources, would the cost of the new one be greater than the cost of adapting the old one?

Pollution. Is this a polluting building?

Energy and location. By what means of transport do users get to the building? Can they walk or are cars used?

Is this a bad area for noise or dirt, so windows can't be opened? Would a replacement building be better placed to mitigate adverse environmental effects?

Ecological. Are there internal issues such as protected bats in the building? Or is this the only attractive green space in an urban environment, for wildlife etc.?

Adaptability. Is it adaptable to changing worship and ministry? To changing standards for heat, light, comfort, safety of staff?
Is it adaptable to providing a workable, efficient, well-laid-out office for staff?
Can it meet the needs of today's working church building?

Summary

To a certain extent there are two key issues when asking whether or not to close a church:

- If it is valued by local people, will they help sustain it financially and in other ways?
- If it is not, can members sustain it by their contributions and build up a viable level of support that can be sustained?

Index

Index